Math Practice

Reinforce and Master

Basic Math Skills

Grades 3–4

Credits

Author: Danette Randolph

Production: Quack & Company, Inc.

Illustrations: Sherry Neidigh

Cover Design: Peggy Jackson

Cover Credits: Photo www.comstock.com

© 1999 EyeWire, Inc. All rights reserved.

ISBN 0-88724-937-X

Table of Contents

Table of Contents

Division

Fractions and Decimals

Graphing, Measurement, and Geometry

Review

Introduction

Math Practice is filled with fun and challenging activities to help students develop and review a wide selection of math skills. Students will practice adding, subtracting, multiplying, and dividing; explore basic geometry concepts; identify fractions and decimals; and much more. Easy-to-follow teaching elements accompany many of the skills. These elements will help build a mathematical foundation for the students. Teachers and parents will find *Math Practice* a valuable tool for helping students achieve growth in their mathematical development.

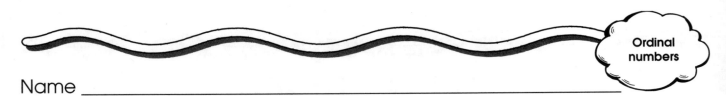

Name _____

First Things First

An **ordinal number** is used to tell order.

Write an ordinal number on each spaceship by counting the spaceship's place in line.

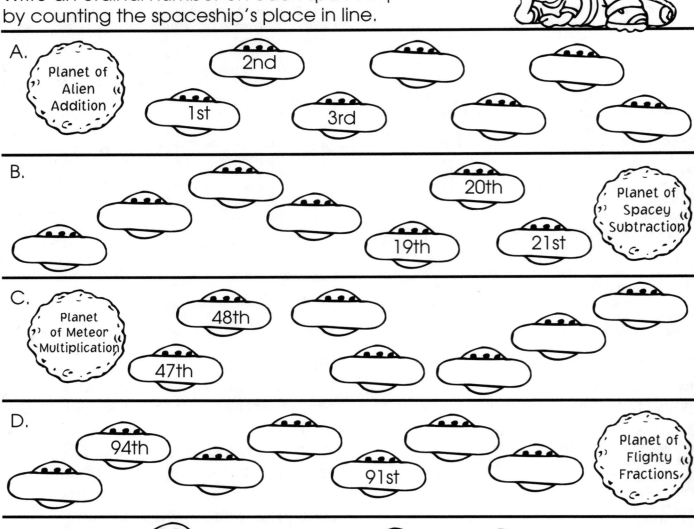

A. Planet of Alien Addition

2nd

1st   3rd

B. 20th

Planet of Spacey Subtraction

19th   21st

C. Planet of Meteor Multiplication

48th

47th

D. 94th

91st

Planet of Flighty Fractions

E. Planet of Invader Decimals

73rd

77th

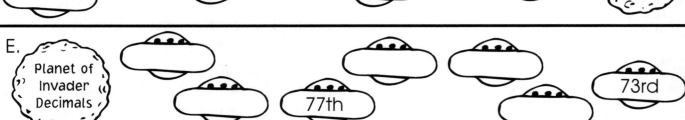

There are 26 aliens flying in space.

If an alien is 17th in line, how many aliens are behind it? ____

How many aliens are ahead of it? ____

Name _____

Silly Space Creatures

Numbers are compared by their value. Words like **same**, **equal**, **more**, **less**, **greater**, **least**, **greatest**, and **fewer** indicate larger or smaller numbers.

Use the clues to finish drawing each silly space creature.

Little Alien

Big Alien

- They have the same number of heads.
- There are three more antennae on each head of the big alien.
- There are two less eyes on each of the little alien's head.
- There are an equal number of mouths on each alien.
- There are three fewer legs on the little alien.
- There are four more arms on the big alien.

 How many more stars are there around the big alien than the little alien? ____

Name _____

Put It in Its Place!

Place value is the value given to the place a digit has in a number. Two-digit numbers have two places.

the **tens column** and the **ones column**

22
2 tens
2 ones

Count the tens and ones. Write the number.

A.		B.		C.		D.	
tens	ones	tens	ones	tens	ones	tens	ones

E.		F.		G.		H.	
tens	ones	tens	ones	tens	ones	tens	ones

 Circle which is greater.

2 tens 9 ones   8 tens 3 ones

Name _____

Juggling Act

Three-digit numbers have three places.

the **hundreds column**, the **tens column**, and the **ones column**

The number in the hundreds column has a greater value than the tens and ones places.

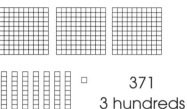

371
3 hundreds
7 tens
1 one

Count the hundreds, tens, and ones. Write the number.

A.
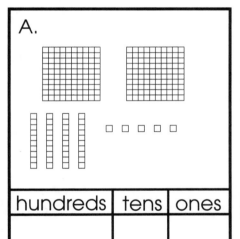

hundreds	tens	ones

B.
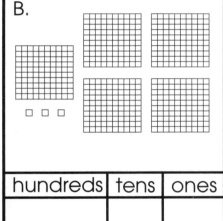

hundreds	tens	ones

C.
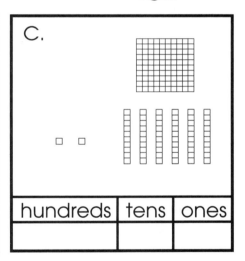

hundreds	tens	ones

D.
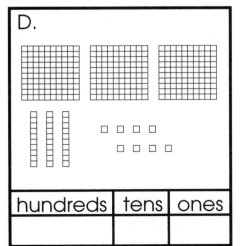

hundreds	tens	ones

E.
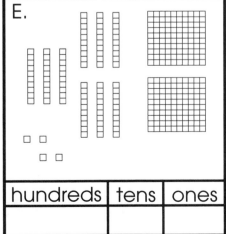

hundreds	tens	ones

F.
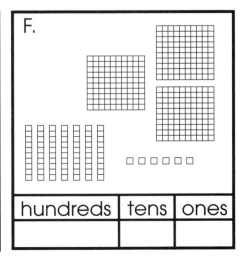

hundreds	tens	ones

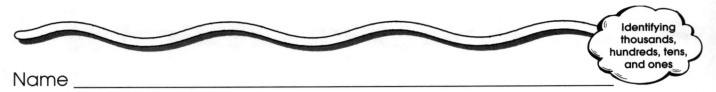
Name _____

Radical Rockets

Four-digit numbers have four places.

the **thousands column**, the **hundreds column**, the **tens column**, and the **ones column**

The number in the thousands column has a greater value than the hundreds, tens, or ones places and is separated with a comma.

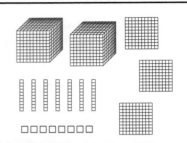

2,478
2 thousands
4 hundreds
7 tens
8 ones

Count the thousands, hundreds, tens, and ones. Draw a line to connect each picture to the correct number.

A.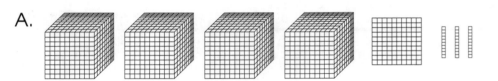

B.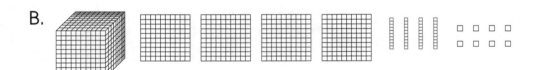

C.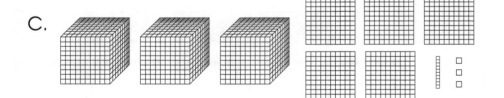

D.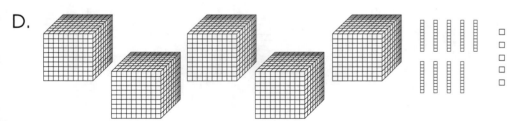

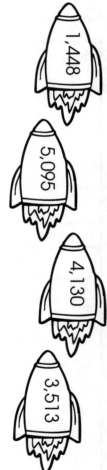

1,448

5,095

4,130

3,513

On another piece of paper, show the year you were born with number blocks.

Name _____

In the Clouds

Numbers can be written in two ways.

Expanded form is a way to write a number that shows the place value of each digit. 2,000 + 200 + 40 + 3

Standard form is a way to write a number that shows only the digits. 2,243

Fill in the missing numbers to complete each number in expanded form and standard form.

	thousands	+	hundreds	+	tens	+	ones		
A.	2,000	+	500	+	80	+	7	=	2,587
B.		+	200	+		+		=	4,__51
C.		+		+		+		=	1,344
D.	6,000	+		+		+		=	__,103
E.		+		+		+	2	=	5,76__
F.		+		+	10	+		=	3,5__0
G.		+		+		+		=	9,475
H.		+		+	30	+		=	7,0__6
I.		+		+		+	0	=	8,65__

Write the number with the most thousands.

Write the number with the least hundreds.

Write the number with no tens.

On another piece of paper, write the year you were born in expanded form.

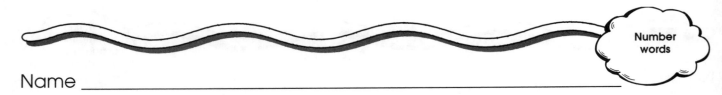

Name _____

Number Names

0, 1, 2, 3, 4, 5, 6, 7, 8, and 9 are **numerals** used to name numbers. Another way to name numbers is with a **number word**.

Read each number word. Use numerals to name each number in the puzzle.

Across

2. forty-five
5. two thousand, sixty-three
7. five hundred thirty-nine
8. one thousand, two hundred eighty-seven
10. five hundred eighty thousand, two hundred forty
11. five thousand, three hundred sixty-nine

Down

1. five hundred four
3. five hundred seventy-two
4. nine hundred sixty thousand, two hundred forty-four
6. eighty-three thousand, twenty-four
9. seven hundred five thousand, nine hundred sixty-one
11. fifty-five

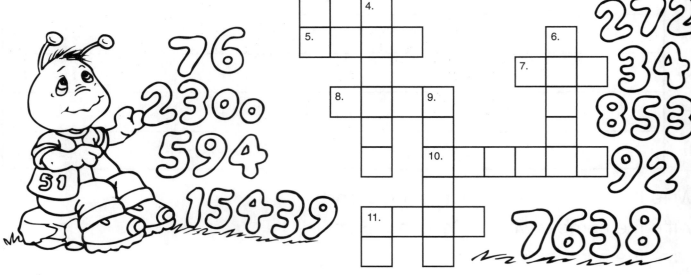

 Write your house or apartment number in words.

_____

Name _____

Sensational Scents

Count by ones to fill in each missing number.

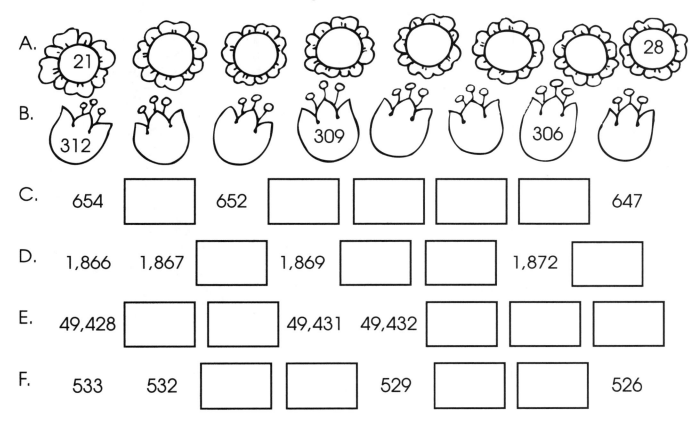

A. 21 28

B. 312 ... ... 309 ... ... 306 ...

C. 654 [ ] 652 [ ] [ ] [ ] 647

D. 1,866 1,867 [ ] 1,869 [ ] [ ] 1,872 [ ]

E. 49,428 [ ] [ ] 49,431 49,432 [ ] [ ] [ ]

F. 533 532 [ ] [ ] 529 [ ] [ ] 526

G. Write the numbers from least to greatest.

5,307
383
246
89,264

H. Write the numbers from greatest to least.

4,178
80,689
4,297
5,150

Name _____

In the Spotlight

An **even** number has 0, 2, 4, 6, or 8 in the ones place and can be divided into two equal groups.

An **odd** number has 1, 3, 5, 7, or 9 in the ones place and cannot be divided into two equal groups.

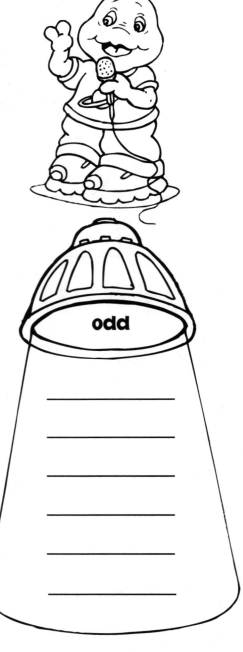

Write each even number in the even spotlight.
Write each odd number in the odd spotlight.

even

52

71,343

6,314

59,870

8,685

97

148

359

569,271

42,936

845

75,244

odd

Circle the correct answer in each sentence.

If you add two even numbers, the sum will be **even/odd**.

If you add two odd numbers, the sum will be **even/odd**.

If you add an even and an odd number, the sum will be **even/odd**.

Name _____

Tree-mendous!

Rounding numbers is a way of replacing one number with another number that tells about how many or how much.

When rounding to the nearest number, look in the column right before it. If that column has 0, 1, 2, 3, or 4 in it, round down. If the column has 5, 6, 7, 8, or 9 in it, round up.

Round 23 to the nearest ten.	Round 284 to the nearest hundred.
Look at the ones digit.	Look at the tens digit.
20 2<u>3</u> 30	200 2<u>8</u>4 300
Round down 23 to 20.	Round up 284 to 300.

Round the numbers on each tree to the place value listed on the trunk.

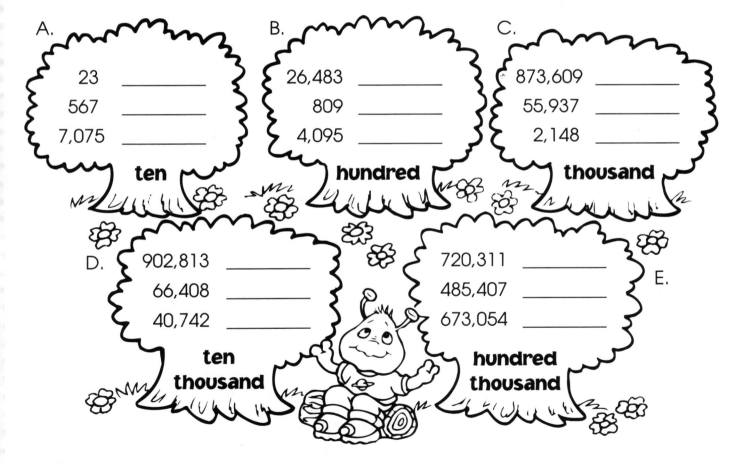

A.
23 _____
567 _____
7,075 _____
ten

B.
26,483 _____
809 _____
4,095 _____
hundred

C.
873,609 _____
55,937 _____
2,148 _____
thousand

D.
902,813 _____
66,408 _____
40,742 _____
ten thousand

E.
720,311 _____
485,407 _____
673,054 _____
hundred thousand

Write five four-digit numbers with a hundreds digit that should be rounded up.

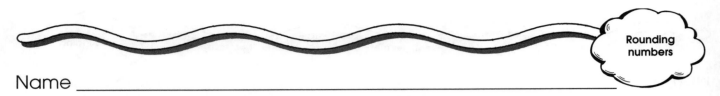

Name _____

Don't Get Dizzy!

Use the underlined digit to round each number.

Example: 4<u>5</u>4 rounds to 500.

86,<u>0</u>00

_____

START

2,7<u>5</u>0

_____

866,<u>2</u>73

_____

9,2<u>5</u>6

_____

1<u>5</u>8,241

_____

3,0<u>8</u>7

_____

99<u>1</u>

_____

56,<u>9</u>24

_____

82

_____

7<u>4</u>,306

_____

2<u>9</u>

_____

7<u>5</u>

_____

9,<u>2</u>80

_____

13,<u>8</u>74

_____

2<u>0</u>4

_____

6<u>0</u>1,557

_____

Write a number that would round to:

3,560 _____   750 _____   30 _____

Name _____

Dare to Compare

To compare numbers is to decide which of two numbers is **greater than** or **less than**.

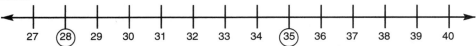

27 (28) 29 30 31 32 33 34 (35) 36 37 38 39 40

If a number is greater than another number, it is farther right on the number line. It is represented by the symbol >.

If a number is less than another number, it is farther left on the number line. It is represented by the symbol <.

28 is **less than** 35	35 is **greater than** 28
28 < 35	35 > 28

If the numbers are on the same spot on the number line, they are equal. This is represented by the symbol =.

Use the symbols **>**, **<** and **=** to compare the numbers.

A. 51 ◯ 31	4,388 ◯ 4,388	21,360 ◯ 21,306
B. 602 ◯ 206	85,104 ◯ 95,104	631,207 ◯ 62,746
C. 2,470 ◯ 2,047	1,347 ◯ 1,374	9,731 ◯ 973
D. 760,355 ◯ 750,366	419 ◯ 411	7,500 ◯ 7,499
E. 6,642 ◯ 66,403	35,267 ◯ 35,267	1,877 ◯ 1,766
F. 300,007 ◯ 300,008	72,380 ◯ 72,387	204,963 ◯ 201,652

Shade each circle with the **greater than** symbol to see what number makes a golfer nervous. _____

Name _____

All Tied Up

Shade the numbers that are described in each box to make a letter. Then, write each letter in order in the spaces below to answer the riddle.

A. greater than 142 and less than 537

536	519	180	242	376
291	100	587	912	511
307	352	475	145	237
486	732	609	946	468
147	86	813	100	299

B. greater than 476 and less than 598

532	498	477	561	590
512	732	313	234	694
575	486	493	504	483
176	853	467	946	559
515	509	525	577	493

C. greater than 42,053 and less than 76,130

48,566	63,103	46,053	53,197	68,310
75,234	42,035	86,000	80,273	74,299
50,246	66,041	53,076	42,100	76,000
43,707	42,026	41,283	56,248	79,245
76,122	76,135	79,201	41,999	76,129

D. greater than 8,904 and less than 11,267

8,907	11,251	10,762	9,341	10,566
11,175	8,901	8,254	11,287	8,943
10,244	11,276	8,903	8,873	9,762
8,914	11,627	11,342	11,269	9,425
9,240	10,560	11,250	10,015	10,617

What kinds of knots are tied in space?

"___ ___ †̲ ___ ___ knots!"

Name _____

Right on Target

Addends are numbers to be added together.

3 + 4

The number that results from adding two or more addends is called the **sum**.

3 + 4 = **7**

Add to complete each target.

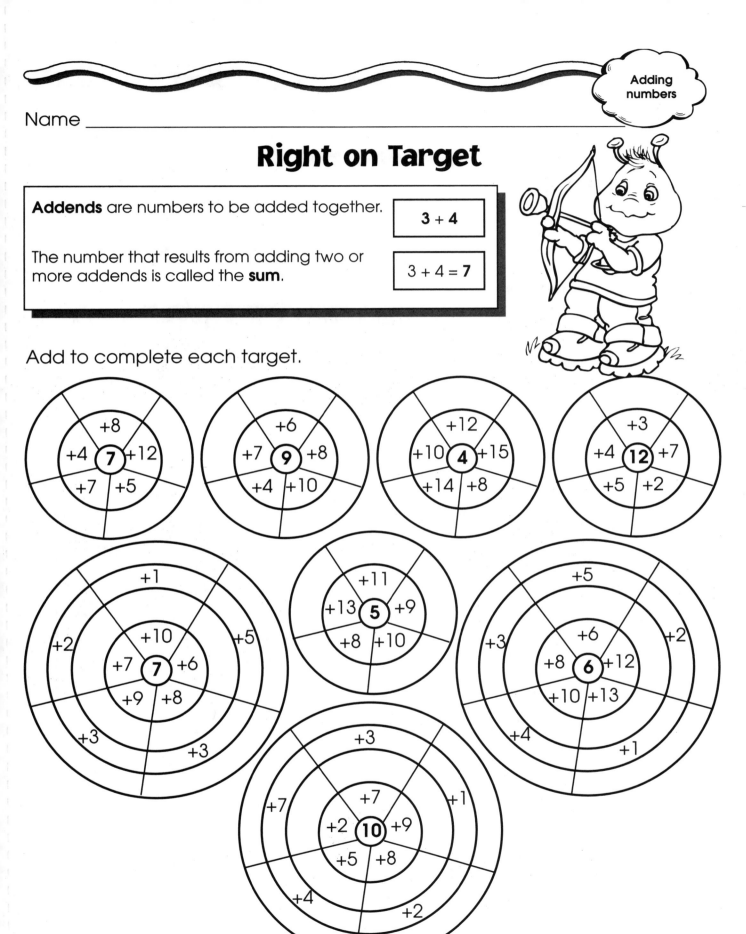

Name _____

Batter Up!

Parentheses show which part of a problem to do first.

$$(12 - 3) + 5 =$$

$$9 + 5 = 14$$

Solve each problem. Complete the problem in the parentheses first. Use the letters to answer the riddle.

$(9 + 9) - 10$	= _____	c	$(6 + 7) - 3$	= _____	h
$(19 - 5) - 8$	= _____	p	$(16 - 11) + 12$	= _____	t
$(2 + 3) + 7$	= _____	n	$(16 - 5) - 8$	= _____	s
$(7 - 4) + 12$	= _____	e	$(18 - 9) - 4$	= _____	y
$(8 + 4) + 2$	= _____	k	$(5 + 6) + 8$	= _____	f
$(13 + 4) - 8$	= _____	b	$(15 - 12) + 8$	= _____	m
$(13 + 3) + 4$	= _____	a	$(7 + 4) + 2$	= _____	q
$(19 - 7) + 6$	= _____	g	$(5 + 6) - 9$	= _____	i
$(20 - 10) - 6$	= _____	r	$(17 - 4) - 6$	= _____	d
$(12 + 8) - 4$	= _____	o	$(13 - 9) + 15$	= _____	l

Why did the baseball team hire a cook?

$\overline{17}$ $\overline{10}$ $\overline{15}$ $\overline{5}$ $\overline{12}$ $\overline{15}$ $\overline{15}$ $\overline{7}$ $\overline{15}$ $\overline{7}$ $\overline{20}$ $\overline{18}$ $\overline{16}$ $\overline{16}$ $\overline{7}$

$\overline{9}$ $\overline{20}$ $\overline{17}$ $\overline{17}$ $\overline{15}$ $\overline{4}$ **!**

Name _____

Three Is a Crowd

To add two-digit numbers, first add the numbers in the ones column. Then add the numbers in the tens column.

$$\begin{array}{r} 2\cancel{3} \\ + \cancel{4}1 \\ \hline 4 \end{array} \qquad \begin{array}{r} \cancel{2}3 \\ + \cancel{4}1 \\ \hline 64 \end{array}$$

Circle the number that does not belong in each sum.
Then, write the letter from the box on the blank that matches the circled number to answer the riddle.

R $\begin{array}{r} 27 \\ + \ 32 \\ \hline 159 \end{array}$	**I** $\begin{array}{r} 12 \\ + \ 62 \\ \hline 764 \end{array}$	**C** $\begin{array}{r} 18 \\ + \ 81 \\ \hline 949 \end{array}$	**P** $\begin{array}{r} 32 \\ + \ 32 \\ \hline 364 \end{array}$	**E** $\begin{array}{r} 84 \\ + \ 15 \\ \hline 929 \end{array}$	**A** $\begin{array}{r} 48 \\ + \ 31 \\ \hline 797 \end{array}$
T $\begin{array}{r} 21 \\ + \ 76 \\ \hline 957 \end{array}$	**A** $\begin{array}{r} 74 \\ + \ 21 \\ \hline 975 \end{array}$	**P** $\begin{array}{r} 61 \\ + \ 28 \\ \hline 893 \end{array}$	**G** $\begin{array}{r} 52 \\ + \ 33 \\ \hline 805 \end{array}$	**P** $\begin{array}{r} 34 \\ + \ 55 \\ \hline 389 \end{array}$	**T** $\begin{array}{r} 52 \\ + \ 15 \\ \hline 657 \end{array}$
C $\begin{array}{r} 33 \\ + \ 44 \\ \hline 774 \end{array}$	**G** $\begin{array}{r} 53 \\ + \ 43 \\ \hline 960 \end{array}$	**R** $\begin{array}{r} 54 \\ + \ 34 \\ \hline 188 \end{array}$	**T** $\begin{array}{r} 33 \\ + \ 52 \\ \hline 585 \end{array}$	**C** $\begin{array}{r} 76 \\ + \ 23 \\ \hline 949 \end{array}$	**R** $\begin{array}{r} 47 \\ + \ 31 \\ \hline 178 \end{array}$

What game can you play at a store?

$\underline{\quad}\ \underline{\quad}\ \underline{\quad}\ \underline{\quad}\ \underline{\quad}\quad \underline{\quad}\ \underline{\quad}\ \underline{\quad}$!
$\ \ \ 3 \quad\ 1 \quad\ \ 6 \quad\ \ 4 \quad\ \ 2 \qquad 5 \quad\ \ 7 \quad\ \ 0$

Name _____

Just Hanging Around

To regroup a number means to name it in a different way. The number 37 can be regrouped into 3 tens and 7 ones.

When adding two-digit numbers, it is sometimes necessary to regroup by carrying tens.

$$
\begin{array}{r}
\overset{1}{5}3 \\
+\ 19 \\
\hline
72
\end{array}
$$

3 + 9 = 12   Regroup the number 12 into 1 ten and 2 ones.

Carry the 1 ten to the tens column. Finish by adding the tens.

Add.

A.

$$
\begin{array}{r} 15 \\ +\ 79 \\ \hline \end{array}
\qquad
\begin{array}{r} 67 \\ +\ 24 \\ \hline \end{array}
\qquad
\begin{array}{r} 19 \\ +\ 85 \\ \hline \end{array}
\qquad
\begin{array}{r} 64 \\ +\ 26 \\ \hline \end{array}
\qquad
\begin{array}{r} 28 \\ +\ 38 \\ \hline \end{array}
\qquad
\begin{array}{r} 71 \\ +\ 19 \\ \hline \end{array}
\qquad
\begin{array}{r} 28 \\ +\ 36 \\ \hline \end{array}
$$

B.

$$
\begin{array}{r} 75 \\ +\ 15 \\ \hline \end{array}
\qquad
\begin{array}{r} 32 \\ +\ 59 \\ \hline \end{array}
\qquad
\begin{array}{r} 89 \\ +\ 15 \\ \hline \end{array}
\qquad
\begin{array}{r} 37 \\ +\ 47 \\ \hline \end{array}
\qquad
\begin{array}{r} 86 \\ +\ 18 \\ \hline \end{array}
\qquad
\begin{array}{r} 46 \\ +\ 17 \\ \hline \end{array}
\qquad
\begin{array}{r} 84 \\ +\ 17 \\ \hline \end{array}
$$

C.

$$
\begin{array}{r} 43 \\ +\ 48 \\ \hline \end{array}
\qquad
\begin{array}{r} 81 \\ +\ 19 \\ \hline \end{array}
\qquad
\begin{array}{r} 53 \\ +\ 28 \\ \hline \end{array}
\qquad
\begin{array}{r} 39 \\ +\ 46 \\ \hline \end{array}
\qquad
\begin{array}{r} 52 \\ +\ 29 \\ \hline \end{array}
\qquad
\begin{array}{r} 78 \\ +\ 17 \\ \hline \end{array}
\qquad
\begin{array}{r} 26 \\ +\ 48 \\ \hline \end{array}
$$

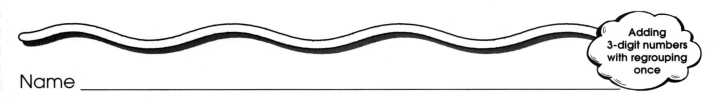

Name _____

Starlight

Add. Shade the sums in the stars. The sums will go across and down.

A.
```
   172        251        326        438        543        682
 + 619      + 319      + 345      + 524      + 348      + 208
```

B.
```
   864        878        791        539        372        291
 + 227      + 108      + 192      + 253      + 484      + 591
```

C.
```
   582        453        382        293        715        382
 + 190      + 219      + 451      + 691      + 235      + 508
```

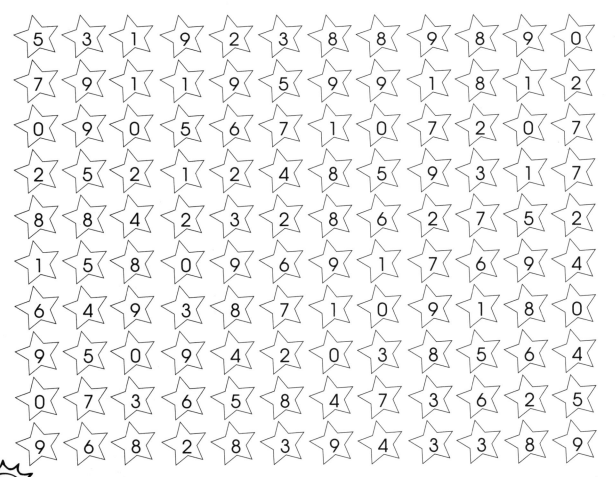

Find three stars in the number find. Write a problem to equal that sum.

Name _____

A Ride in Space

Add. Draw an **X** on each square with a sum that has a 3 in the ones place to make a path to the spaceship.

	189 + 246	238 + 576	347 + 254	477 + 183
526 + 197 327 + 296	664 + 236	753 + 148	821 + 189	319 + 283
178 + 178 185 + 638	268 + 193	247 + 257	366 + 478	458 + 477
727 + 183 637 + 286	594 + 159	816 + 586	915 + 786	345 + 777
234 + 596 353 + 287	475 + 438	236 + 789	684 + 188	765 + 476
897 + 385 173 + 897	959 + 654	544 + 679	124 + 599	278 + 675

On another piece of paper, write a problem with a sum of 333 with two three-digit numbers using regrouping.

Adding 4-digit numbers with regrouping once

Name ______________________________

Time to Rise

Add.

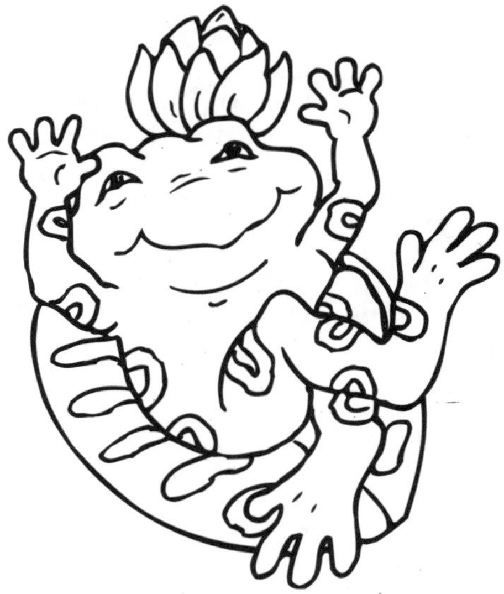

1,898 + 4,071 **T**	3,379 + 2,720 **H**	4,132 + 1,473 **A**		
5,753 + 1,239 **C**	7,412 + 1,238 **K**	2,027 + 7,457 **F**		
8,645 + 1,148 **D**	9,461 + 1,219 **n**	2,091 + 5,374 **R**	3,526 + 4,339 **O**	7,916 + 1,973 **A**
6,281 + 2,914 **O**	4,735 + 1,258 **T**	5,263 + 1,164 **E**	6,054 + 2,528 **A**	8,307 + 2,137 **W**

Write the sums from least to greatest and the letter with it to find out when frogs wake up.

5,605 / ___ / ___ / ___ / ___ / ___ / ___ / ___ / ___ / ___ / ___ / ___ / ___ / ___ / ___ / ___

A □   □□□   □□□□□   □□   □□□□!

Name _____

Break the Chain

Add. Look at the sums in each chain to find a similarity. Draw an **X** on the sum that does not have the similarity found in the chain of sums.

A.

$$1,532 + 4,278$$ $$7,157 + 1,473$$ $$4,368 + 3,552$$ $$2,496 + 3,277$$ $$3,774 + 3,166$$

B.

$$1,307 + 1,496$$ $$3,285 + 1,516$$ $$2,743 + 7,058$$ $$6,422 + 2,379$$ $$5,416 + 2,385$$

C.

$$1,705 + 8,197$$ $$2,596 + 7,247$$ $$3,681 + 6,179$$ $$4,874 + 5,058$$ $$3,209 + 4,198$$

D.

$$1,374 + 3,874$$ $$3,846 + 4,671$$ $$4,957 + 2,562$$ $$5,637 + 3,882$$ $$6,568 + 1,950$$

On another piece of paper, create a chain of similar sums.

Name _____

Tricky Business

Add. Write the letter that matches each sum below to find what kind of jokes mathematicians play.

$$\begin{array}{r} 8,713 \\ + 1,487 \\ \hline \end{array}$$
A

$$\begin{array}{r} 3,708 \\ + 4,597 \\ \hline \end{array}$$
C

$$\begin{array}{r} 2,647 \\ + 1,778 \\ \hline \end{array}$$
S

$$\begin{array}{r} 4,036 \\ + 1,997 \\ \hline \end{array}$$
E

$$\begin{array}{r} 9,424 \\ + 1,896 \\ \hline \end{array}$$
R

$$\begin{array}{r} 4,541 \\ + 4,859 \\ \hline \end{array}$$
T

$$\begin{array}{r} 4,332 \\ + 3,769 \\ \hline \end{array}$$
I

$$\begin{array}{r} 6,529 \\ + 1,685 \\ \hline \end{array}$$
M

$$\begin{array}{r} 3,057 \\ + 1,967 \\ \hline \end{array}$$
K

$$\begin{array}{r} 1,215 \\ + 4,789 \\ \hline \end{array}$$
H

10,200	11,320	8,101	9,400	6,004	8,214	6,033	9,400	11,320	8,101	8,305	5,024	4,425

Math Practice: Grades 3–4

Name _____

Sail Away

Add. Write the letter that matches each sum below to find how you mail a boat.

63,458
+ 10,157   **J**

64,295
+ 29,621   **R**

83,619
+ 13,573   **M**

18,091
+ 34,354   **y**

46,344
+ 19,636   **S**

53,418
+ 49,438   **T**

27,376
+ 25,470   **P**

78,432
+ 13,149   **o**

38,183
+ 14,284   **I**

44,486
+ 47,383   **H**

36,453
+ 45,482   **u**

68,089
+ 17,109   **!**

You ___ ___ ___ ___ **it!**
65,980   91,869   52,467   52,846

Math Practice: Grades 3–4

Name _____

Apple Picking

Use the numbers on the apples to complete the problem on each basket.

Name _____

Take Cover

Add. Use the sums to complete the puzzle.

Across

1.
$$\begin{array}{r} 47,365 \\ + \ 38,778 \\ \hline \end{array}$$

4.
$$\begin{array}{r} 74,507 \\ + \ 19,899 \\ \hline \end{array}$$

6.
$$\begin{array}{r} 18,056 \\ + \ 25,947 \\ \hline \end{array}$$

7.
$$\begin{array}{r} 15,078 \\ + \ 16,995 \\ \hline \end{array}$$

9.
$$\begin{array}{r} 27,551 \\ + \ 29,579 \\ \hline \end{array}$$

10.
$$\begin{array}{r} 25,107 \\ + \ 16,893 \\ \hline \end{array}$$

Down

1.
$$\begin{array}{r} 28,566 \\ + \ 52,879 \\ \hline \end{array}$$

2.
$$\begin{array}{r} 16,547 \\ + \ 18,467 \\ \hline \end{array}$$

3.
$$\begin{array}{r} 47,618 \\ + \ 34,685 \\ \hline \end{array}$$

5.
$$\begin{array}{r} 37,085 \\ + \ 25,958 \\ \hline \end{array}$$

8.
$$\begin{array}{r} 30,854 \\ + \ 39,666 \\ \hline \end{array}$$

Name _____

Great Set of Wheels

Add. Draw an **X** on each box with an even sum. Write the letters of each odd sum in order on the lines below.

4,362 47 103 + 1,231 **(A)**	2,015 1,788 502 + 81 **(R)**	8,230 466 23 + 599 **(U)**	556 23 1,672 + 430 **(C)**
5,176 245 29 + 1,350 **(E)**	2,340 88 106 + 3,443 **(A)**	279 3,100 83 + 466 **(S)**	4,173 2,050 664 + 88 **(R)**
6,208 752 410 + 3,345 **(P)**	73 89 501 + 6,245 **(M)**	4,037 288 54 + 3,901 **(X)**	330 1,471 206 + 5,188 **(O)**
2,701 1,527 64 + 5 **(O)**	2,376 104 24 + 731 **(L)**	3,042 187 1,822 + 11 **(D)**	505 2,367 21 + 283 **(F)**

What do you call a car filled with water?

___ ___ ___ ___ ___ ___ ___ ___

Name _____

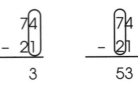

Cast a Line

The number that results from subtracting one number from another is called the **difference**.

$$7 - 3 = 4 \qquad 7 - 4 = 3$$

To subtract two-digit numbers, first subtract the numbers in the ones column. Then subtract the numbers in the tens column.

$$\begin{array}{r} 74 \\ -\ 21 \\ \hline 3 \end{array} \qquad \begin{array}{r} 74 \\ -\ 21 \\ \hline 53 \end{array}$$

Subtract.

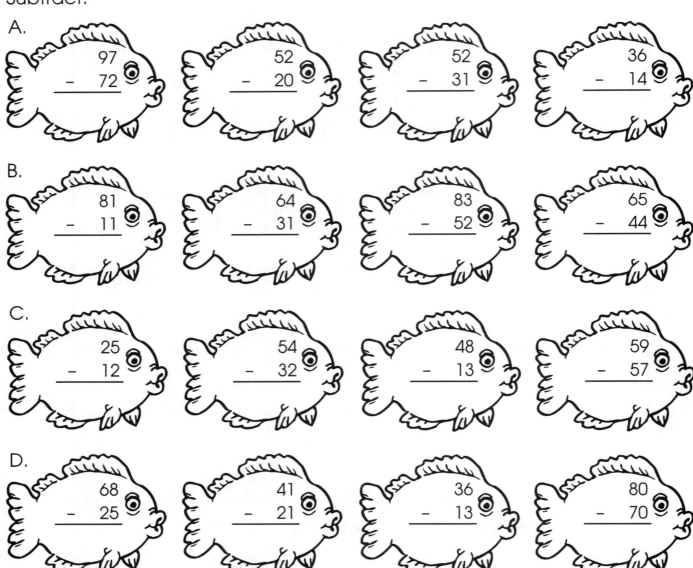

A.

$$\begin{array}{r} 97 \\ -\ 72 \\ \hline \end{array} \qquad \begin{array}{r} 52 \\ -\ 20 \\ \hline \end{array} \qquad \begin{array}{r} 52 \\ -\ 31 \\ \hline \end{array} \qquad \begin{array}{r} 36 \\ -\ 14 \\ \hline \end{array}$$

B.

$$\begin{array}{r} 81 \\ -\ 11 \\ \hline \end{array} \qquad \begin{array}{r} 64 \\ -\ 31 \\ \hline \end{array} \qquad \begin{array}{r} 83 \\ -\ 52 \\ \hline \end{array} \qquad \begin{array}{r} 65 \\ -\ 44 \\ \hline \end{array}$$

C.

$$\begin{array}{r} 25 \\ -\ 12 \\ \hline \end{array} \qquad \begin{array}{r} 54 \\ -\ 32 \\ \hline \end{array} \qquad \begin{array}{r} 48 \\ -\ 13 \\ \hline \end{array} \qquad \begin{array}{r} 59 \\ -\ 57 \\ \hline \end{array}$$

D.

$$\begin{array}{r} 68 \\ -\ 25 \\ \hline \end{array} \qquad \begin{array}{r} 41 \\ -\ 21 \\ \hline \end{array} \qquad \begin{array}{r} 36 \\ -\ 13 \\ \hline \end{array} \qquad \begin{array}{r} 80 \\ -\ 70 \\ \hline \end{array}$$

Math Practice: Grades 3–4

Name _____

Knights of the Number Table

Sometimes it is necessary to regroup when subtracting two-digit numbers. If the number being subtracted in the ones column is too big, borrow a ten and regroup it into 10 ones.

$$\begin{array}{r} \overset{4\;13}{\cancel{5}\cancel{3}} \\ -\;16 \\ \hline 37 \end{array}$$

6 is too big to take away from 3.
Borrow a ten and regroup it into 10 ones.
Subtract the ones column.
Subtract the tens column.

Subtract. Add the digits in each difference. If the sum of the digits equals 9, write the letter on the blank below.

85 − 26	65 − 29	76 − 38	91 − 27
G	**S**	**D**	**A**
52 − 23	47 − 19	38 − 19	96 − 28
M	**C**	**L**	**J**
83 − 38	78 − 49	64 − 47	53 − 35
W	**B**	**n**	**O**
44 − 17	57 − 28	61 − 34	72 − 58
R	**H**	**D**	**E**

What is a knight's favorite fish to eat?

___ ___ ___ ___ ___ **fish**

Name _____

Can You See It?

Subtract. Shade each difference in the chart. The differences will go across and down.

A.

257	419	368	643	758	827
− 108	− 127	− 185	− 170	− 284	− 344

B.

936	291	466	673	385	824
− 275	− 103	− 237	− 358	− 159	− 244

4	1	4	9	3	2	9	2	2	1	5	1
9	0	7	8	6	1	2	2	9	4	0	3
1	7	3	1	5	0	5	9	8	2	7	6
3	5	2	6	7	4	9	4	8	7	1	0
7	7	5	3	9	3	2	1	8	8	4	3
0	4	8	6	8	1	3	8	9	3	7	7
5	0	9	2	9	0	5	9	6	2	4	2
6	1	4	5	2	1	8	4	2	7	1	8
4	2	8	3	0	3	0	5	7	1	3	0
1	8	3	6	5	4	6	8	6	9	4	7
7	9	6	1	1	6	2	3	7	2	2	3
2	2	6	3	2	4	5	6	5	8	4	1
8	0	1	3	4	5	6	1	4	5	0	9

C.

525	917
− 283	− 623

D.

427	632
− 156	− 271

E.

913	367
− 208	− 183

F.

542	754
− 180	− 361

Name _____

Go for a Strike

Sometimes it is necessary to regroup tens and hundreds when subtracting three-digit numbers.

$$\begin{array}{r} {}^{3\ 13} \\ \$\ 6.4\!\!\!/3\!\!\!/ \\ -\ \$\ 2.58 \\ \hline \$\ \quad 5 \end{array}$$

8 is too big to take away from 3.
Borrow a ten and regroup it into 10 ones.
Subtract the ones column.

5 is too big to take away from 3.
Borrow a hundred and regroup it into 10 tens.
Subtract the tens column.
Subtract the hundreds column.

$$\begin{array}{r} {}^{5\ 13\ 13} \\ \$\ 6.4\!\!\!/3\!\!\!/ \\ -\ \$\ 2.58 \\ \hline \$\ 3.85 \end{array}$$

When subtracting money, remember to use a decimal point (.) and a dollar sign ($) in the difference.

Subtract. Then, use the letter code to answer the riddle below.

K $ 3.81 – $ 1.93	**Y** $ 3.72 – $ 1.95	**E** $ 4.68 – $ 2.79	**B** $ 5.53 – $ 1.69
I $ 6.18 – $ 2.39	**R** $ 7.23 – $ 4.58	**C** $ 8.16 – $ 3.77	**O** $ 9.45 – $ 7.66
S $ 8.57 – $ 3.98	**U** $ 7.43 – $ 4.55	**T** $ 6.34 – $ 2.57	**H** $ 5.27 – $ 1.38

How do you win money bowling?

‾‾‾‾‾ ‾‾‾‾‾ ‾‾‾‾‾   ‾‾‾‾‾ ‾‾‾‾‾ ‾‾‾‾‾ ‾‾‾‾‾ ‾‾‾‾‾ ‾‾‾‾‾
$1.77 $1.79 $2.88 $4.59 $3.77 $2.65 $3.79 $1.88 $1.89

!

‾‾‾‾‾ ‾‾‾‾‾   ‾‾‾‾‾ ‾‾‾‾‾ ‾‾‾‾‾ ‾‾‾‾‾
$3.79 $3.77 $2.65 $3.79 $4.39 $3.89

Name _____

In the Box

Subtract. In the puzzle, write a number word for the numeral in each box.

Across				
3. 8,145 − 5,721 ☐	5. 4,658 − 1,823 ☐	8. 4,586 − 2,469 ☐	9. 3,994 − 2,905 ☐	12. 5,819 − 3,742 ☐

Down

1. 3,458 − 1,275 ☐	
2. 9,245 − 2,722 ☐	
3. 6,722 − 1,590 ☐	4. 8,647 − 6,935 ☐
6. 8,371 − 2,080 ☐	7. 4,574 − 1,764 ☐
10. 9,497 − 3,521 ☐	11. 7,263 − 4,158 ☐

Name _____

Pelican Patterns

Subtract. Match the pattern of the differences in each row to the correct fish.

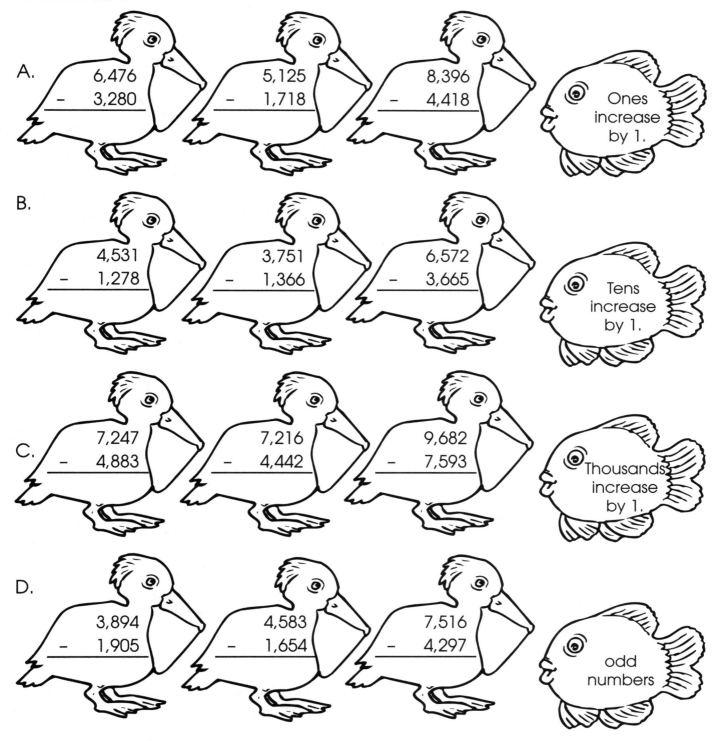

A.
$$6,476 - 3,280$$ $$5,125 - 1,718$$ $$8,396 - 4,418$$

Ones increase by 1.

B.
$$4,531 - 1,278$$ $$3,751 - 1,366$$ $$6,572 - 3,665$$

Tens increase by 1.

C.
$$7,247 - 4,883$$ $$7,216 - 4,442$$ $$9,682 - 7,593$$

Thousands increase by 1.

D.
$$3,894 - 1,905$$ $$4,583 - 1,654$$ $$7,516 - 4,297$$

odd numbers

Name _____

nothing but net

Subtract. Write the letter that matches each difference below to find what illness you might get from playing basketball.

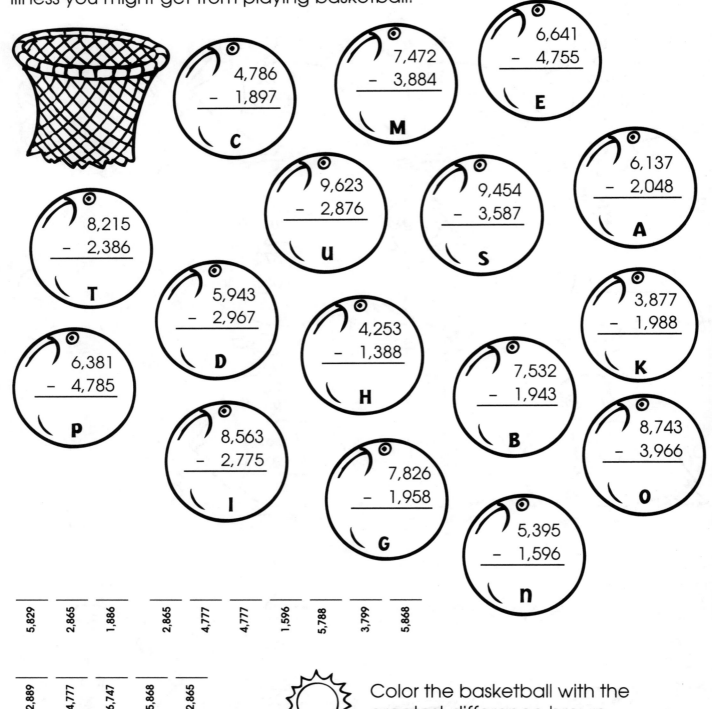

$$\begin{array}{r} 4,786 \\ -\ 1,897 \\ \hline \end{array}$$ C

$$\begin{array}{r} 7,472 \\ -\ 3,884 \\ \hline \end{array}$$ M

$$\begin{array}{r} 6,641 \\ -\ 4,755 \\ \hline \end{array}$$ E

$$\begin{array}{r} 9,623 \\ -\ 2,876 \\ \hline \end{array}$$ u

$$\begin{array}{r} 9,454 \\ -\ 3,587 \\ \hline \end{array}$$ S

$$\begin{array}{r} 6,137 \\ -\ 2,048 \\ \hline \end{array}$$ A

$$\begin{array}{r} 8,215 \\ -\ 2,386 \\ \hline \end{array}$$ T

$$\begin{array}{r} 5,943 \\ -\ 2,967 \\ \hline \end{array}$$ D

$$\begin{array}{r} 4,253 \\ -\ 1,388 \\ \hline \end{array}$$ H

$$\begin{array}{r} 3,877 \\ -\ 1,988 \\ \hline \end{array}$$ K

$$\begin{array}{r} 6,381 \\ -\ 4,785 \\ \hline \end{array}$$ P

$$\begin{array}{r} 7,532 \\ -\ 1,943 \\ \hline \end{array}$$ B

$$\begin{array}{r} 8,563 \\ -\ 2,775 \\ \hline \end{array}$$ I

$$\begin{array}{r} 8,743 \\ -\ 3,966 \\ \hline \end{array}$$ O

$$\begin{array}{r} 7,826 \\ -\ 1,958 \\ \hline \end{array}$$ G

$$\begin{array}{r} 5,395 \\ -\ 1,596 \\ \hline \end{array}$$ n

5,829 2,865 1,886 2,865 4,777 4,777 1,596 5,788 3,799 5,868

2,889 4,777 6,747 5,868 2,865

Color the basketball with the greatest difference brown.

Name _____

Get the Clues

Subtract. Then, color each box by following the clues below.

63,848 − 31,939	84,737 − 41,488	65,226 − 32,307	26,815 − 13,096
97,154 − 55,426	78,963 − 55,774	59,672 − 47,285	68,381 − 24,653
77,432 − 61,604	86,453 − 42,538	75,574 − 32,386	81,495 − 24,327
61,616 − 23,407	74,357 − 38,724	51,248 − 23,622	92,069 − 73,459

Blue
- forty-one thousand, seven hundred twenty-eight
- 2,000 more than 13,828

Green
- 82,734 backward
- 5 ten thousands

Red
- 40 less than 43,289
- 32,922, 32,921, 32,920, _____

Orange
- 300 less than 35,933
- twenty-seven thousand, six hundred twenty-six

Yellow
- thirty-one thousand, nine hundred nine
- 6 hundreds and 0 ones
- 6,000 less than 18,387
- forty-three thousand, nine hundred fifteen
- 50 less than 38,259
- 200 less than 13,919
- 100 more than 23,089
- 43,186, 43,187, _____

Name _____

Get into Shape

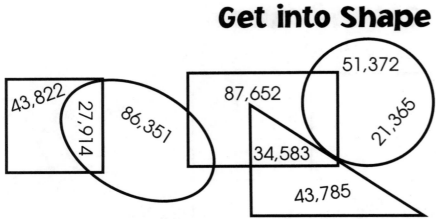

43,822   27,914   86,351   87,652   51,372   21,365   34,583   43,785

Find the difference for each pair of numbers listed.

A. the numbers in the rectangle	B. the larger number in the square and the larger number in the triangle
C. the smaller number in the circle and the larger number in the triangle	D. the smaller number in the triangle and the smaller number in the circle
E. the larger number in the circle and the smaller number in the rectangle	F. the larger number in the square and the larger number in the oval
G. the larger number in the square and the smaller number in the circle	H. the larger number in the circle and smaller number in the oval

Find the sum of all the numbers in the shapes above.

_____

Name _____

Let's Pal Around

A number **palindrome** is a number that reads the same forward or backward.

232   1,441   457,754

Subtract. Circle each difference that is a number palindrome.

A.
$$94,623 - 66,754$$ $$81,542 - 22,757$$

B.
$$27,834 - 19,955$$ $$45,882 - 17,994$$

C.
$$95,381 - 66,599$$ $$68,365 - 49,576$$ $$82,518 - 24,679$$ $$78,671 - 39,788$$

D.
$$23,476 - 19,888$$ $$33,257 - 17,378$$ $$51,771 - 33,889$$ $$64,121 - 35,739$$

On another piece of paper, write a five-digit palindrome. Then, write a subtraction problem with the palindrome as the difference.

Name _____

Help Needed

Sometimes it is necessary to regroup with 0. If there is a 0 in the place from which you need to borrow, go to the next column.

$$\begin{array}{r} \overset{4\ \ 9\ 10}{\cancel{500}} \\ -\ 284 \\ \hline 216 \end{array}$$

Borrow 1 hundred and regroup it into 10 tens.
Borrow 1 ten and regroup it into 10 ones.
Subtract.

Subtract. Write the letter that matches each difference below to answer the riddle.

430 − 155	950 − 471	2,054 − 1,662	603 − 325	6,033 − 3,750
S	**A**	**R**	**n**	**B**
502 − 133	40,309 − 12,179	30,508 − 12,399	20,707 − 10,948	401 − 174
o	**I**	**u**	**c**	**T**

What can you do to help mathematicians with their back problems?

Put them in

___ ___ ___ − ___ ___ ___ ___ ___ ___ ___ ___

275   18,109   2,283   227   392   479   9,759   227   28,130   369   278

Name _____

Tip the Scales

Subtract. Draw an **X** on the larger difference.

```
   500          700
 - 273        - 266
```

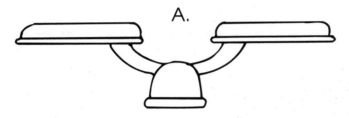

A.

```
  2,000        4,000
- 1,342      - 1,533
```

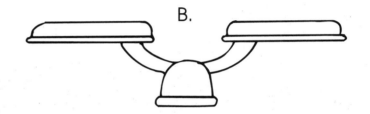

B.

```
  6,000        5,000
- 2,475      - 1,355
```

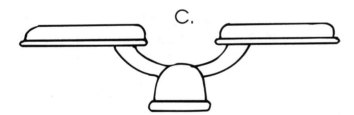

C.

```
  60,000       90,000
- 25,462     - 64,215
```

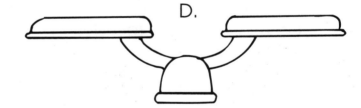

D.

```
  8,000        6,000
- 4,468      - 1,577
```

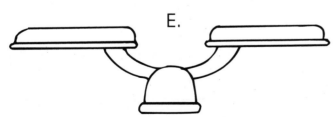

E.

```
  70,000       30,000
- 45,433     - 19,216
```

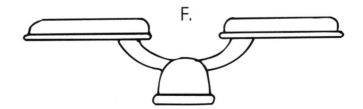

F.

Subtract the year you were born from the year it is now.

Name _____

Dash to the Diner

Write each problem. Add or subtract. Be sure to include a decimal point and a dollar sign in your answer.

A. Kirk bought a pizza for $7.62. He gave the clerk $20.00. How much change did he receive?	$20.00 – $ 7.62
B. Dean bought French fries and paid $5.00. He received $3.37 in change. How much were the French fries?	
C. Andrew is buying a soda. A large soda costs $2.43 and a medium soda costs $1.85. How much more does the large soda cost?	
D. David paid $1.37 for a hamburger, $2.76 for a salad, and 99¢ for a soda. How much did he pay altogether?	
E. Jordan and Joel will share a lunch. Jordan has $4.66 and Joel has $3.75. Can they share a pizza for $8.25?	
F. Jamie bought an ice-cream cone for $1.49. Then, she bought a shake for $3.76. How much did she spend altogether?	

If you have $5.00, how many pretzels can you buy for $1.25?

Name _____

Crazy Cricket Counting

Write the missing numbers on each line.

A. Count by twos.

4, 6, ____ , ____ , ____ , 14, ____ , ____ , ____ , ____

B. Count by fives.

10, ____ , 20, ____ , ____ , 35, ____ , ____ , ____

C. Count by fours.

4, 8, ____ , ____ , 20, ____ , ____ , 32, ____ , 40

D. Count by threes.

3, 6, 9, ____ , ____ , ____ , ____ , 24, ____ , ____

E. Count by sixes.

6, 12, 18, ____ , ____ , 36, ____ , ____ , 54, ____

F. Count by nines.

9, 18, ____ , ____ , ____ , 54, ____ , 72, ____ , ____

G. Count by eights.

8, 16, 24, ____ , ____ , ____ , 56, ____ , ____ , 80

H. Count by sevens.

7, 14, ____ , ____ , ____ , 42, 49, ____ , ____ , ____

 Count by your age.

____ , ____ , ____ , ____ , ____ ,

43
Math Practice: Grades 3–4

Name _____

Sets of Flying Saucers

Multiplication is a quick way to add. It tells the total number when equal sets are put together.

Factors are numbers multiplied together. The first factor tells the number of sets. The second factor tells the number in each set.

$$3 + 3 = 6$$
2 sets of 3 equals 6
$$2 \times 3 = 6$$

Add. Then, multiply.

A.

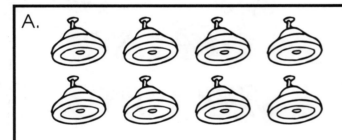

___ + ___ + ___ + ___ = ___

___ sets of ___ equals ___

___ x ___ = ___

B.

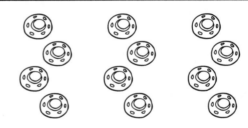

___ + ___ + ___ = ___

___ sets of ___ equals ___

___ x ___ = ___

C.

___ + ___ + ___ + ___ + ___ = ___

___ sets of ___ equals ___

___ x ___ = ___

D.

___ + ___ + ___ +

___ + ___ + ___ = ___

___ sets of ___ equals ___

___ x ___ = ___

Math Practice: Grades 3–4

Name _____

Out of This World

The number that results from multiplying two factors is called the **product**.

Use the pictures to find the product.

A.

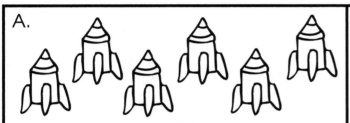

___ rockets x ___ legs = ___ legs

___ x ___ = ___

B.

___ planets x ___ moons = ___ moons

___ x ___ = ___

C.

___ spaceships x ___ aliens = ___ aliens

___ x ___ = ___

D.

___ cases x ___ food tubes = ___ food tubes

___ x ___ = ___

E.

___ moons x ___ craters = ___ craters

___ x ___ = ___

F.

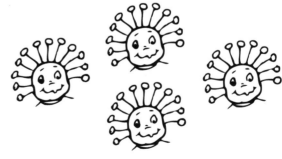

___ aliens x ___ antennae = ___ antennae

___ x ___ = ___

Name _____

Turn It Around

The product is the same even if the factors are turned around.

2 x 3 = 6

3 x 2 = 6

Draw a line to connect the facts with the same factors. Then, draw a line to the product of the two facts.

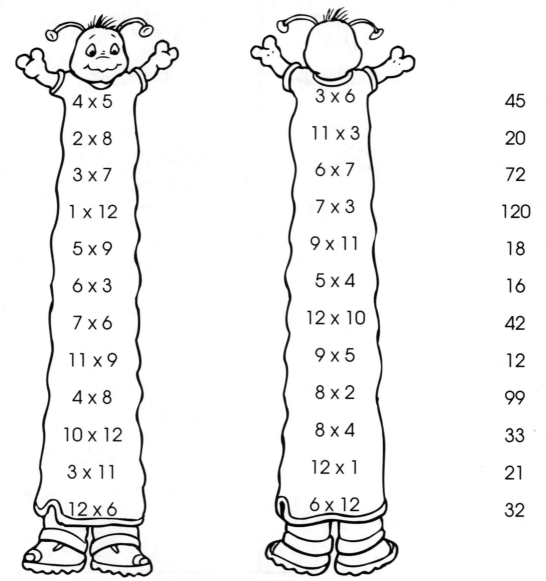

4 x 5	3 x 6	45
2 x 8	11 x 3	20
3 x 7	6 x 7	72
1 x 12	7 x 3	120
5 x 9	9 x 11	18
6 x 3	5 x 4	16
7 x 6	12 x 10	42
11 x 9	9 x 5	12
4 x 8	8 x 2	99
10 x 12	8 x 4	33
3 x 11	12 x 1	21
12 x 6	6 x 12	32

Math Practice: Grades 3–4

Name _____

Get the Facts

Multiply to complete each chart.

A.

	x 2
7	
12	
4	
8	
5	

B.

	x 5
2	
5	
8	
3	
9	

C.

	x 10
4	
9	
10	
3	
5	

D.

	x 8
8	
7	
11	
3	
5	

E.

	x 4
4	
9	
12	
5	
3	

F.

	x 6
12	
4	
11	
8	
7	

G.

	x 9
3	
12	
8	
6	
2	

H.

	x 3
12	
7	
11	
6	
9	

I.

	x 7
8	
12	
7	
6	
9	

J.

	x 12
3	
7	
6	
5	
4	

K.

	x 11
9	
4	
2	
7	
6	

On another piece of paper, find the sum of the products in each box.

Color the chart with the greatest sum yellow.

Color the chart with the smallest sum green.

Name _____

Zooming Zero

Multiply. Trace the car's path to the finish line by following products with a zero.

2 x 5	8 x 5	4 x 0	10 x 12	6 x 9	3 x 7
12 x 2	1 x 11	5 x 5	4 x 5	7 x 8	9 x 9
4 x 9	9 x 1	12 x 7	0 x 3	4 x 4	2 x 8
11 x 6	3 x 8	6 x 4	5 x 6	10 x 8	8 x 6
9 x 7	2 x 3	11 x 8	7 x 7	2 x 10	1 x 3
5 x 3	8 x 2	3 x 12	6 x 8	9 x 0	12 x 5

Write 10 multiplication facts with 4 in the product.

Name _____

Fill It Up

Multiply to complete the chart.

X	0	1	2	3	4	5	6	7	8	9	10	11	12
0													
1													
2													
3													
4													
5													
6													
7													
8													
9													
10													
11													
12													

A. Color the product of double factors red.

B. Complete each sentence.

Multiples of zero always equal ____ .

Multiples of ten always end with ____ .

Multiples of five always end with ____ or ____ .

C. Write **even** or **odd** in each blank.

even number x even number =_____ number

odd number x odd number = _____ number

even number x odd number = _____ number

Name _____

America the Beautiful

To multiply a two-digit number by a one-digit number, first multiply the number in the ones column by the number. Then, multiply the number in the tens column by the number.

$$\begin{array}{r} 24 \\ \times\ 2 \\ \hline 8 \end{array} \qquad \begin{array}{r} 24 \\ \times\ 2 \\ \hline 48 \end{array}$$

Fill in the missing number to complete each problem. Then, write the letter that matches each number below to answer the riddle.

A
$$\begin{array}{r} \square 6 \\ \times\ \ \ 1 \\ \hline 7\ 6 \end{array}$$

M
$$\begin{array}{r} 9\square \\ \times\ \ \ 2 \\ \hline 1\ 8\ 8 \end{array}$$

T
$$\begin{array}{r} 1\square \\ \times\ \ \ 4 \\ \hline 4\ 8 \end{array}$$

E
$$\begin{array}{r} \square 2 \\ \times\ \ \ 2 \\ \hline 1\ 6\ 4 \end{array}$$

Q
$$\begin{array}{r} \square 1 \\ \times\ \ \ 4 \\ \hline 2\ 4\ 4 \end{array}$$

S
$$\begin{array}{r} \square 1 \\ \times\ \ \ 8 \\ \hline 8\ 8 \end{array}$$

U
$$\begin{array}{r} 5\ 2 \\ \times\ \ \ 4 \\ \hline 2\ \square\ 8 \end{array}$$

I
$$\begin{array}{r} 2\ 3 \\ \times\ \ \ 3 \\ \hline 6\ \square \end{array}$$

R
$$\begin{array}{r} 3\square \\ \times\ \ \ 2 \\ \hline 6\ 6 \end{array}$$

What is a mathematician's favorite spot in America?

<u> 2 </u> <u> 9 </u> <u> 4 </u> <u> 8 </u> <u> 1 </u> <u> 1 </u> <u> 6 </u> <u> 0 </u> <u> 7 </u> <u> 3 </u> <u> 8 </u>

Name _____

Born to Fly

Sometimes it is necessary to regroup when multiplying two-digit numbers by one number. Regroup by carrying tens.

$$\overset{2}{2}8 \quad 8 \times 3 = 24$$
$$\underline{\times 3}$$
$$84$$

Regroup the number 24 into 2 tens and 4 ones.

Carry the 2 tens to the tens column.

Multiply the tens column. ($2 \times 3 = 6$)

Then, add the carried tens. ($6 + 2 = 8$)

Multiply.

A.
```
   18          59
x   2       x   9
```

B.
```
   92          47
x   7       x   9
```

C.
```
   83          27
x   4       x   3
```

D.
```
   16          52
x   2       x   8
```

E.
```
   93          38
x   5       x   4
```

F.
```
   79          24
x   7       x   3
```

G.
```
   83          93
x   4       x   5
```

H.
```
   72          64
x   6       x   6
```

I.
```
   66          65
x   8       x   6
```

A dozen is equal to 12. Write the total number for each amount.

2 dozen	5 dozen	8 dozen	4 dozen	7 dozen
12 x 2				

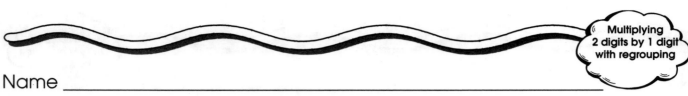
Name _____

Park It

Multiply. Draw a line to match each car with its parking space by connecting matching products.

A.
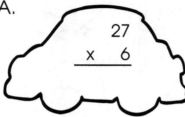

    27
x   6

B.
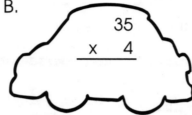

    35
x   4

C.
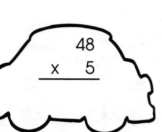

    48
x   5

D.
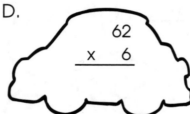

    62
x   6

E.
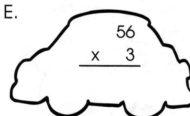

    56
x   3

F.
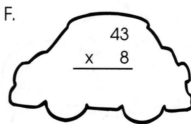

    43
x   8

G.
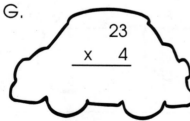

    23
x   4

    28
x   5

    54
x   3

    46
x   2

    93
x   4

    30
x   8

    86
x   4

    28
x   6

On another piece of paper, write two multiplication problems with matching products.

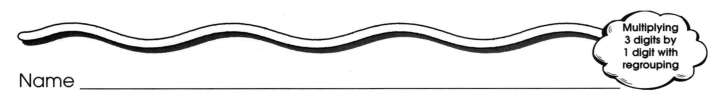

Search and Find

Multiply. Circle each product in the puzzle. The products will go across and down.

A.
$$192 \times 2$$ $$547 \times 3$$ $$435 \times 2$$ $$216 \times 3$$ $$385 \times 4$$

B.
$$554 \times 2$$ $$372 \times 8$$ $$652 \times 8$$ $$864 \times 3$$ $$188 \times 5$$

C.
$$943 \times 4$$ $$398 \times 6$$

D.
$$857 \times 2$$ $$213 \times 7$$

E.
$$436 \times 5$$ $$724 \times 6$$

F.
$$953 \times 8$$ $$789 \times 7$$

G.
$$862 \times 9$$ $$579 \times 5$$

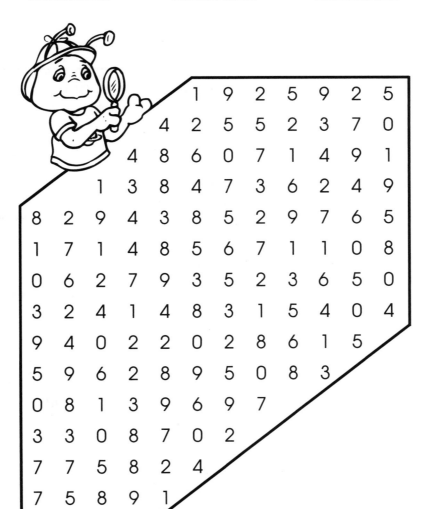

```
    1 9 2 5 9 2 5
    4 2 5 5 2 3 7 0
  4 8 6 0 7 1 4 9 1
  1 3 8 4 7 3 6 2 4 9
8 2 9 4 3 8 5 2 9 7 6 5
1 7 1 4 8 5 6 7 1 1 0 8
0 6 2 7 9 3 5 2 3 6 5 0
3 2 4 1 4 8 3 1 5 4 0 4
9 4 0 2 2 0 2 8 6 1 5
5 9 6 2 8 9 5 0 8 3
0 8 1 3 9 6 9 7
3 3 0 8 7 0 2
7 7 5 8 2 4
7 5 8 9 1
2 3 7
```

Math Practice: Grades 3–4

Name _____

Shopping for Snacks

Remember to use a **decimal point** (.) and a **dollar sign** ($) in the product.

Solve each problem.

How much will it cost for . . .

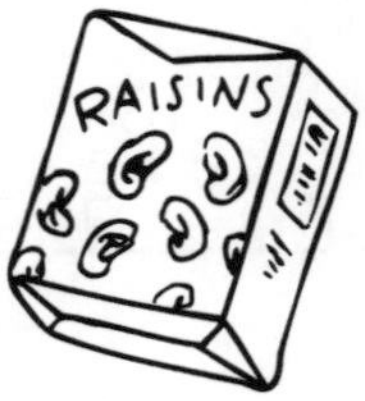

RAISINS
$1.17

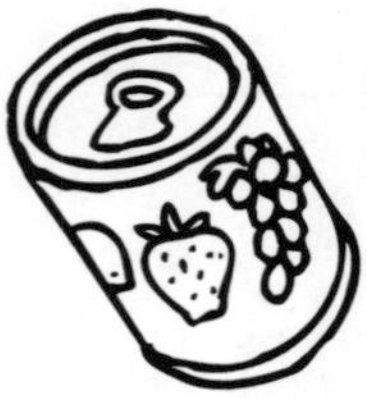

$2.59

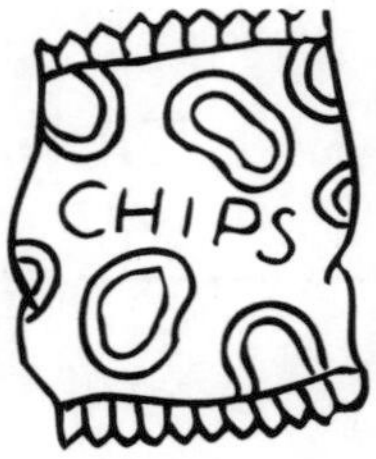

CHIPS
$3.62

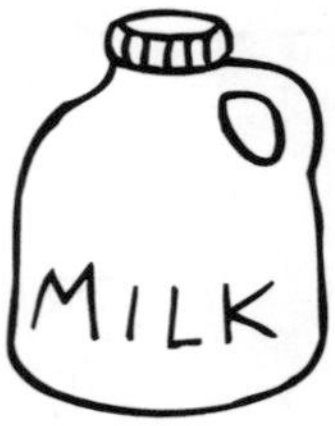

MILK
$3.46

A. 3 boxes of raisins?	B. 8 packs of gum?
$ 1.17 $\underline{\qquad 3}$	
C. 2 loaves of bread?	D. 5 boxes of cereal?
E. 4 gallons of milk?	F. 7 bags of chips?
G. 9 cans of juice?	H. 6 bags of fruit?

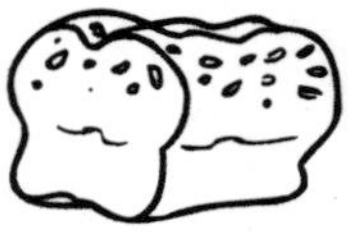

$2.35

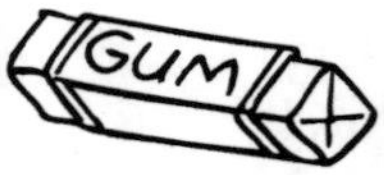

GUM
$1.07

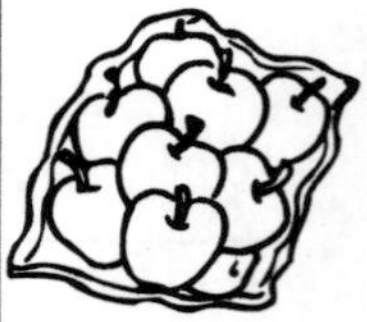

$6.47

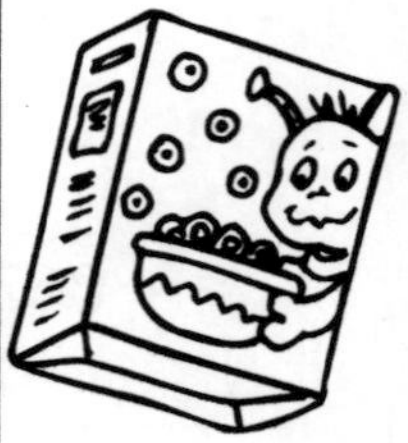

$3.73

Name _____

Share a Smile

Sometimes it is necessary to regroup when multiplying four-digit numbers by one number. Regroup by carrying ones to tens, tens to hundreds, and hundreds to thousands.

Multiply. Use the products to complete the puzzle.

Across

1.
```
  9,042
x     6
```

3.
```
  9,423
x     5
```

4.
```
  3,698
x     6
```

6.
```
  7,955
x     5
```

8.
```
  3,480
x     6
```

9.
```
  7,134
x     4
```

Down

2.
```
  6,153
x     4
```

4.
```
  6,347
x     4
```

5.
```
  2,796
x     3
```

7.
```
  5,132
x     9
```

8.
```
  2,804
x     8
```

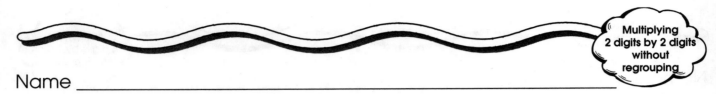

Name _____

Get into Shape

To multiply a two-digit number by another two-digit number, first multiply each digit by the ones column.

$$\begin{array}{r} 2\,3 \\ \times\ 1\,2 \\ \hline 6 \end{array} \longrightarrow \begin{array}{r} 2\,3 \\ \times\ 1\,2 \\ \hline 4\,6 \end{array}$$

Next, put a 0 in the ones column under the 6. Then, multiply each digit by the tens column.

$$\begin{array}{r} 2\,3 \\ \times\ 1\,2 \\ \hline 4\,6 \\ 0 \end{array} \quad \begin{array}{r} 2\,3 \\ \times\ 1\,2 \\ \hline 4\,6 \\ 3\,0 \end{array} \quad \begin{array}{r} 2\,3 \\ \times\ 1\,2 \\ \hline 4\,6 \\ 2\,3\,0 \end{array}$$

Last, add the two products together.

$$\begin{array}{r} 2\,3 \\ \times\ 1\,2 \\ \hline 4\,6 \\ +\ 2\,3\,0 \\ \hline 2\,7\,6 \end{array}$$

Use the symbols to solve each problem.

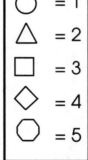

□ = 0
○ = 1
△ = 2
□ = 3
◇ = 4
⬡ = 5

A.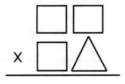

B.

C.

Name _____

Shark Snacks

Sometimes it is necessary to regroup when multiplying a two-digit number by another two-digit number.

Multiply by the ones digit. Regroup as needed.

$$\begin{array}{r} \overset{2}{3}7 \\ \times\ 24 \\ \hline 148 \end{array}$$

Put a 0 in the ones column. Multiply by the tens digit.

$$\begin{array}{r} \overset{1}{3}7 \\ \times\ 24 \\ \hline 148 \\ 740 \end{array}$$

Add the products together.

$$\begin{array}{r} 37 \\ \times\ 24 \\ \hline 148 \\ +\ 740 \\ \hline 888 \end{array}$$

Multiply. Then, write the letter that matches each product below to answer the riddle.

E
74
x 44

K
35
x 76

J
97
x 22

A
82
x 78

W
69
x 52

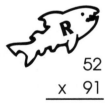

R
52
x 91

S
47
x 23

B
94
x 89

E
28
x 96

A
67
x 75

What should you feed a mean, hungry shark?

___ ___ ___ ___ ___ ___ ___ ___ ___ ___ ___ !
2,134 6,396 3,588 8,366 4,732 3,256 6,396 2,660 3,256 4,732 1,081

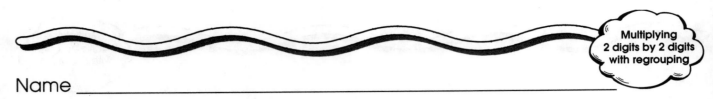

Name _____

A Great Mix

Multiply. Then, write the letter that matches each product below to answer the riddle.

A 18 x 24	F 82 x 37	S 65 x 45
y 32 x 75	G 19 x 68	L 40 x 87
c 77 x 36	E 30 x 97	I 98 x 38
u 78 x 46	n 47 x 35	R 55 x 54

What do you get when you cross a spaceship and a chef?

_____ _____ _____ _____ _____ _____ _____   _____ _____ _____ _____ _____ _____
432   3,034   3,480   2,400   3,724   1,645   1,292   2,925   432   3,588   2,772   2,910   2,970

Name _____

Double Delight

Multiply.

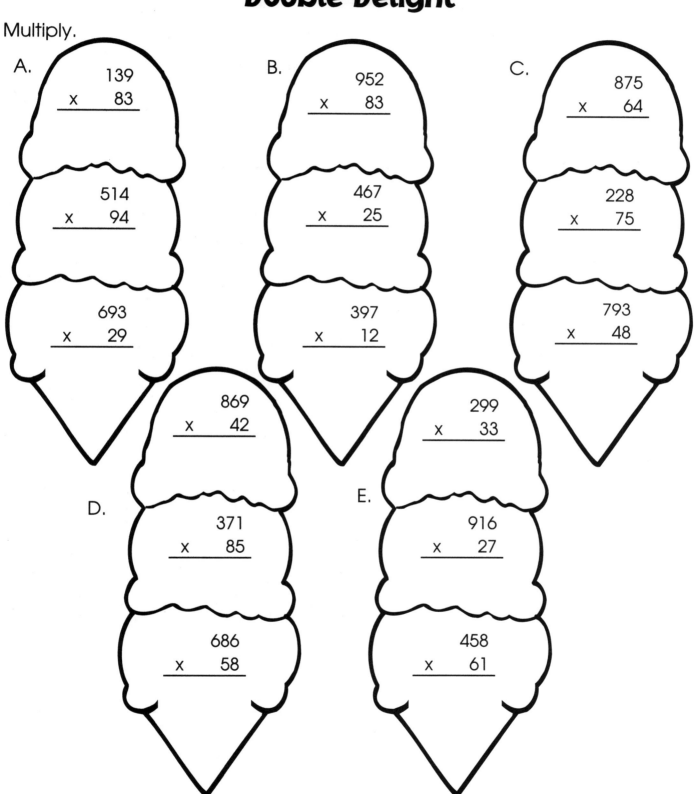

A.
139
x   83

514
x   94

693
x   29

B.
952
x   83

467
x   25

397
x   12

C.
875
x   64

228
x   75

793
x   48

D.
869
x   42

371
x   85

686
x   58

E.
299
x   33

916
x   27

458
x   61

Name _____

A Perfect Punt

Multiply. Write the letter that matches each number below to answer the riddle.

P	**U**	**B**	**O**
941	832	727	694
x 28	x 53	x 86	37

E	**R**	**n**	**L**
580	416	245	268
x 45	x 74	x 88	x 23

I	**W**	**S**	**A**
353	386	561	437
x 56	x 67	x 77	x 83

Where does a football player enjoy eating cereal?

"_____ _____ _____   "_____ _____ _____ _____ _____   _____ _____ _____ _____

19,768   21,560   36,271   43,197   44,096   26,348   26,100   30,784   62,522   25,678   25,862   6,164

Name _____

Time to Review

Fill in the circle beside the correct answer.

1. four thousand, eight hundred sixty-two

   Ⓐ 4,682   Ⓑ 4,268   Ⓒ 4,862   Ⓓ 4,826

2. thirty-seven thousand, five hundred one

   Ⓐ 37,510   Ⓑ 37,501   Ⓒ 37,051   Ⓓ 370,501

3. Round 2,376 to the nearest ten. _____

4. Round 65,485 to the nearest hundred. _____

5. Round 258,374 to the nearest thousand. _____

Fill in the circle beside the correct symbol.

6. 3,642 ◯ 3,624   Ⓐ >   Ⓑ <   Ⓒ =

7. 78,990 ◯ 78,995   Ⓐ >   Ⓑ <   Ⓒ =

Solve.

8. $(12 + 5) - 8 =$ _____

9. $(18 - 4) - 7 =$ _____

10. $5 + (11 - 3) =$ _____

11. $10 + (6 + 4) =$ _____

Name _____

12.   264
   +   188

13.   3,909
  + 2,497

14.   48,556
  + 27,485

15.   35,247
     609
   1,882
  +   23

16.   88
  − 29

17.   582
  − 197

18.   7,213
  − 4,448

19.   387
  + 56

Name _____

20.
```
   908
-  245
```

21.
```
   8,004
-  1,538
```

22.
```
   37
x   4
```

23.
```
   76
x   9
```

24.
```
   582
x    8
```

25.
```
   6,407
x      9
```

26.
```
   95
x  34
```

27.
```
   307
x    85
```

28.
```
   556
x   24
```

29.
```
   53,992
-  17,999
```

Name _____

Fruitful Work

Division tells how many groups can be made from
a given set or how many items are in each set.

Use the picture to fill in each blank.

A.

____ apples in all

____ bowls of apples

____ apples in each bowl

16 divided by 4 equals 4

____ ÷ ____ = ____

B.

____ bananas in all

____ bunches of bananas

____ bananas in each bunch

12 divided by 4 equals 3

____ ÷ ____ = ____

C.

____ grapes in all

____ stems of grapes

____ grapes on each stem

70 divided by 7 equals 10

____ ÷ ____ = ____

D.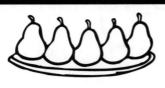

____ pears in all

____ plates of pears

____ pears on each plate

15 divided by 3 equals 5

____ ÷ ____ = ____

Name _____

Spacey Sets

The **dividend** is the number to be divided in a division sentence. It tells the total number of items.

The **divisor** is the number by which a dividend is divided. It tells the number in each set.

The **quotient** is the number that is the result of dividing. It tells the number of sets.

$$\text{divisor} \overline{) \text{dividend}}^{\text{quotient}}$$

$$3\overline{)18}^{6}$$

Write each missing number.

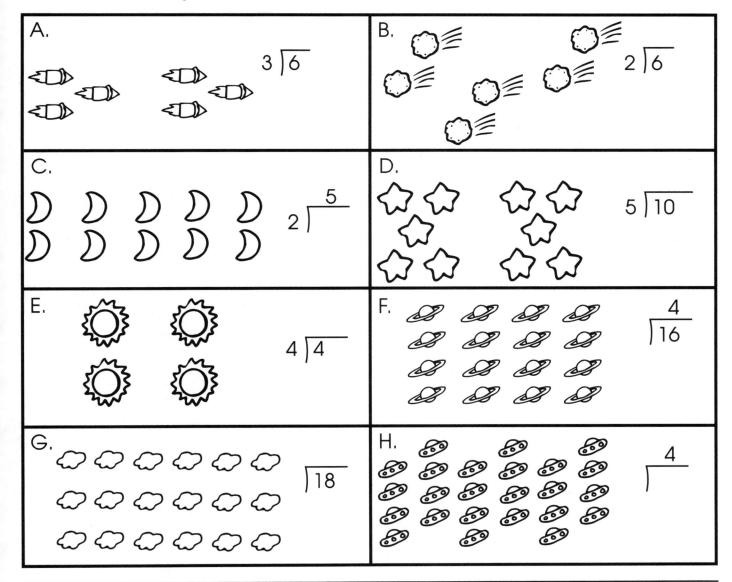

Name _____

Happy Families

A **fact family** is a group of related multiplication and division facts that uses the same set of numbers.

$3 \times 4 = 12$
$4 \times 3 = 12$ Knowing multiplication facts
$12 \div 4 = 3$ helps with division!
$12 \div 3 = 4$

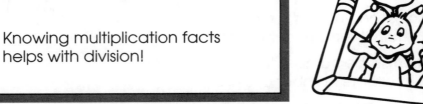

Use the numbers to make a family of related facts.

A.
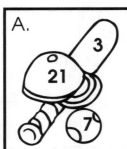
3   21   7

___ x ___ = ___
___ x ___ = ___
___ ÷ ___ = ___
___ ÷ ___ = ___

B.
6   48   8

___ x ___ = ___
___ x ___ = ___
___ ÷ ___ = ___
___ ÷ ___ = ___

C.

56   7   8

___ x ___ = ___
___ x ___ = ___
___ ÷ ___ = ___
___ ÷ ___ = ___

D.
9   36   4

___ x ___ = ___
___ x ___ = ___
___ ÷ ___ = ___
___ ÷ ___ = ___

E.   **5, 20, 4**

___ x ___ = ___
___ x ___ = ___
___ ÷ ___ = ___
___ ÷ ___ = ___

F.   **18, 2, 9**

___ x ___ = ___
___ x ___ = ___
___ ÷ ___ = ___
___ ÷ ___ = ___

G.   **8, 3, 24**

___ x ___ = ___
___ x ___ = ___
___ ÷ ___ = ___
___ ÷ ___ = ___

H.   **7, 5, 35**

___ x ___ = ___
___ x ___ = ___
___ ÷ ___ = ___
___ ÷ ___ = ___

  Write another fact family.

Name _____

Dive into Division

Divide.

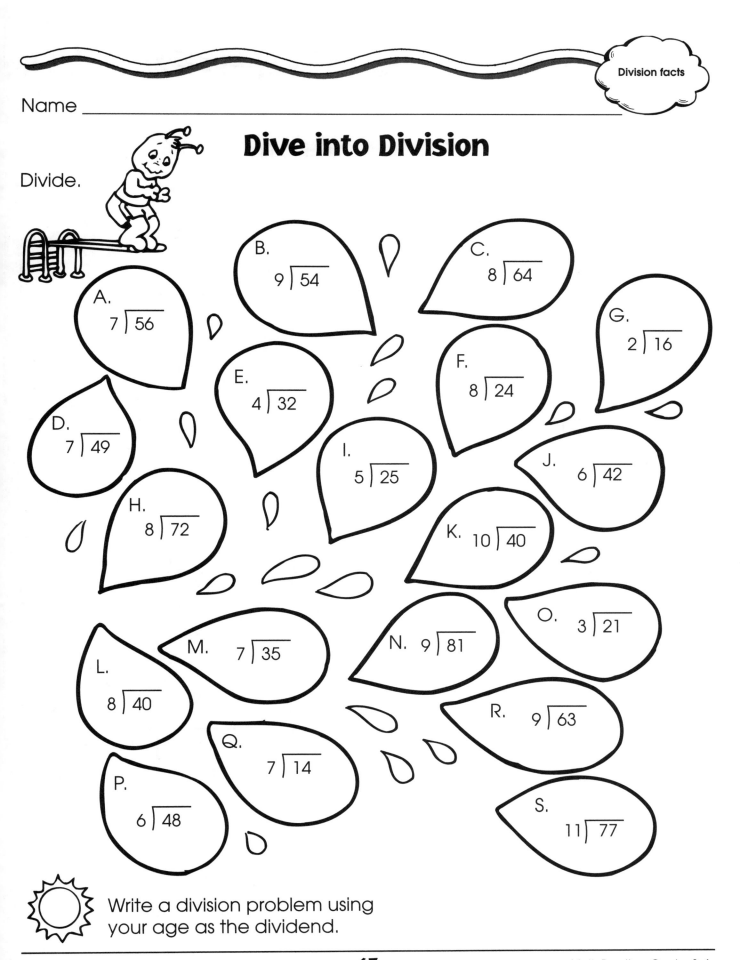

B.
$9 \overline{)54}$

C.
$8 \overline{)64}$

G.
$2 \overline{)16}$

A.
$7 \overline{)56}$

F.
$8 \overline{)24}$

E.
$4 \overline{)32}$

D.
$7 \overline{)49}$

I.
$5 \overline{)25}$

J.
$6 \overline{)42}$

H.
$8 \overline{)72}$

K. $10 \overline{)40}$

O. $3 \overline{)21}$

M. $7 \overline{)35}$

N. $9 \overline{)81}$

L.
$8 \overline{)40}$

R. $9 \overline{)63}$

Q.
$7 \overline{)14}$

P.
$6 \overline{)48}$

S.
$11 \overline{)77}$

Write a division problem using your age as the dividend.

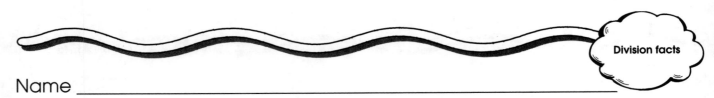

Name _____

Dandy Division

Divide. Shade the triangle with the correct quotient.

A.

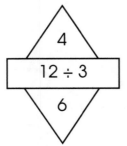

4
12 ÷ 3
6

7
28 ÷ 4
6

8
63 ÷ 7
9

8
27 ÷ 3
9

7
7 ÷ 1
1

B.

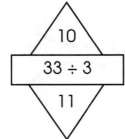

10
33 ÷ 3
11

5
12 ÷ 2
6

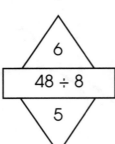

6
48 ÷ 8
5

2
10 ÷ 5
5

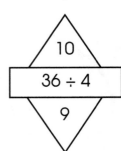

10
36 ÷ 4
9

C.

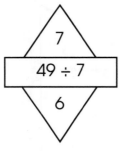

7
49 ÷ 7
6

8
81 ÷ 9
9

11
40 ÷ 4
10

5
35 ÷ 7
4

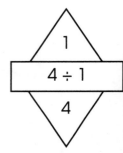

1
4 ÷ 1
4

D.

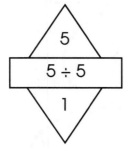

5
5 ÷ 5
1

4
24 ÷ 6
5

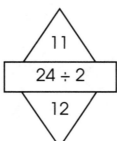

11
24 ÷ 2
12

7
42 ÷ 6
8

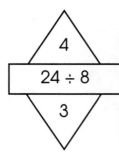

4
24 ÷ 8
3

Four friends want to share 24 cookies. Write a division problem to find the number of cookies each friend will eat.

Name _____

The Giant Mammal

To divide a two-digit dividend by a
one-digit divisor, use these steps.

First, see if the tens digit is big enough to
divide into. If yes, divide. Then, multiply the
partial quotient by the divisor and subtract.

Next, bring down the ones digit with
the difference.

Last, divide the divisor into that number,
multiply, and subtract.

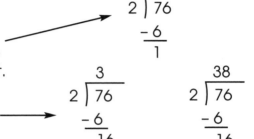

$$2\overline{)76} \quad \begin{array}{r} 3 \\ \hline -6 \\ \hline 1 \end{array}$$

$$2\overline{)76} \quad \begin{array}{r} 3 \\ \hline -6 \\ \hline 16 \end{array} \qquad 2\overline{)76} \quad \begin{array}{r} 38 \\ \hline -6 \\ \hline 16 \\ -16 \\ \hline 0 \end{array}$$

Divide. Connect the dots with numbers from least to greatest.

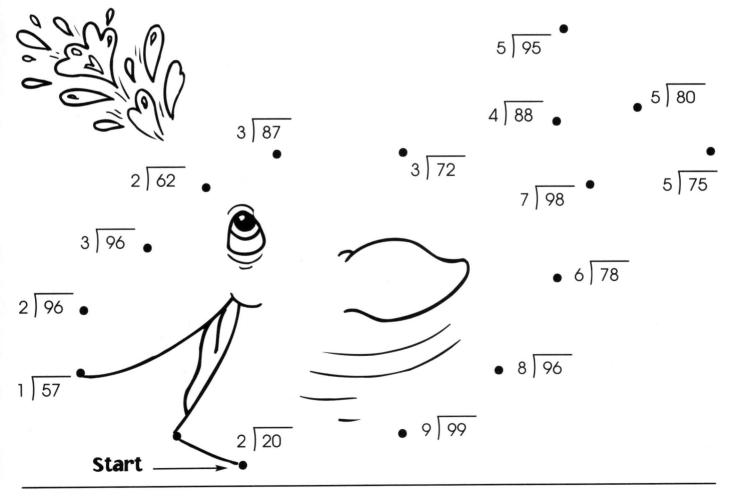

$5\overline{)95}$

$4\overline{)88}$

$5\overline{)80}$

$3\overline{)87}$

$3\overline{)72}$

$5\overline{)75}$

$2\overline{)62}$

$7\overline{)98}$

$3\overline{)96}$

$6\overline{)78}$

$2\overline{)96}$

$8\overline{)96}$

$1\overline{)57}$

$2\overline{)20}$

$9\overline{)99}$

Start ⟶

Name _____

Tissue, Please!

To divide three-digit dividends by a one-digit divisor, first see if the hundreds digit is large enough to divide into. If yes, divide. Then, multiply the partial quotient by the divisor and subtract.

Second, bring down the number in the tens digit with the difference.

Third, divide the divisor into that number, multiply, and subtract.

Last, bring down the number in the ones digit with the difference, divide the divisor into that number, multiply, and subtract.

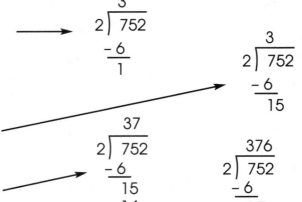

Divide. Write the letter that matches each quotient below to answer the riddle.

E 6)978   **R** 7)938   **L** 3)591   **B** 5)695   **E** 4)676

H 4)712   **U** 5)880   **A** 2)918   **W** 3)891   **B** 3)792

Have you ever seen a fish cry?

L 4)952   **B** 2)538

No, but I have seen a ___ ___ ___ ___ ___
　　　　　　　　　　　297　178　459　238　169

___ ___ ___ ___ ___ ___ ___ !
139　197　176　269　264　163　134

Name _____

Flying High

Divide.

A. 2) 7,956

B. 6) 8,874

C. 3) 7,935

D. 7) 8,918

E. 4) 7,476

F. 8) 9,952

H. 5) 9,735

I. 7) 9,961

G. 3) 8,517

Name _____

Gum Balls Galore

Sometimes the first digit in the dividend is not large enough to divide into. Move to the next digit in the dividend. Divide into that two-digit dividend, multiply, and subtract.

```
        9
    4 ) 36
      - 36
        0
```

```
         34
     6 ) 204
       - 18
         24
       - 24
         0
```

Divide.

5) 435

7) 455

3) 237

8) 752

7) 252

4) 372

8) 128

5) 295

7) 546

5) 495

7) 385

9) 855

3) 261

4) 336

5) 375

2) 178

3) 195

7) 399

6) 186

2) 146

Math Practice: Grades 3–4

Name _____

A Beautiful Note

Divide.

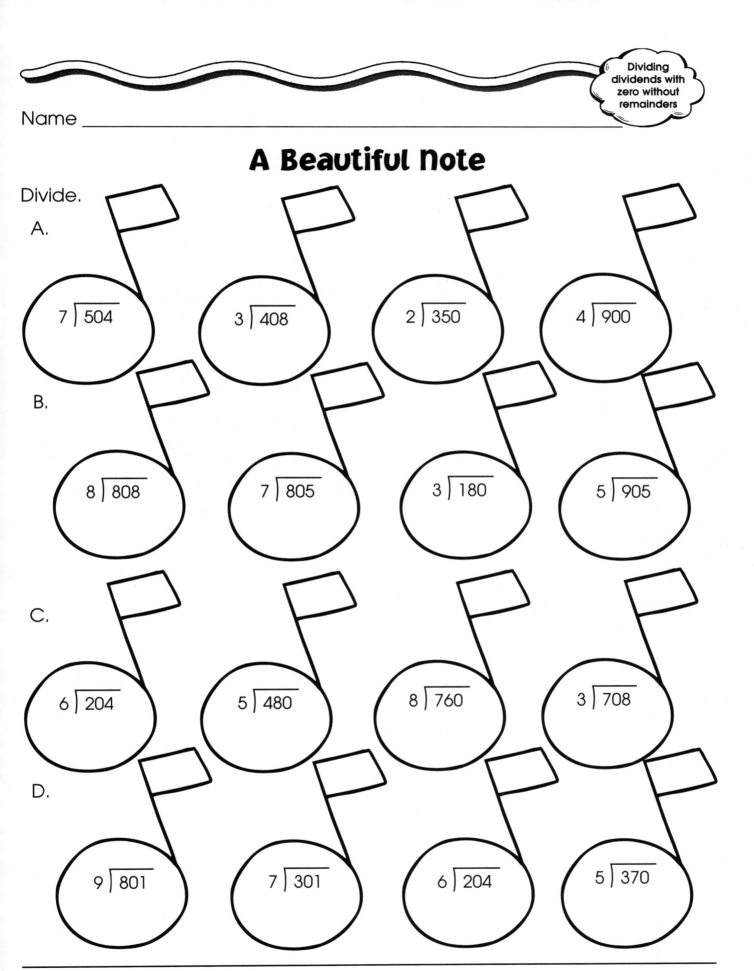

A.

$7\overline{)504}$ $3\overline{)408}$ $2\overline{)350}$ $4\overline{)900}$

B.

$8\overline{)808}$ $7\overline{)805}$ $3\overline{)180}$ $5\overline{)905}$

C.

$6\overline{)204}$ $5\overline{)480}$ $8\overline{)760}$ $3\overline{)708}$

D.

$9\overline{)801}$ $7\overline{)301}$ $6\overline{)204}$ $5\overline{)370}$

Name _____

Leftovers

Sometimes it is necessary to name a remainder when dividing. The **remainder** is the number remaining after the division is complete.

3 cannot divide into 2. There are no more digits to bring down from the dividend. The difference becomes the remainder (R). ⟶

$$
\begin{array}{r}
29\ R2 \\
3\overline{)89} \\
-6 \\
\hline
29 \\
-27 \\
\hline
2
\end{array}
$$

Divide. Write the letter that matches each remainder below to answer the riddle.

What do rattlesnakes like to learn about most in school?

H $2\overline{)19}$ K $7\overline{)40}$ O $8\overline{)76}$ Y $5\overline{)38}$

L $3\overline{)18}$ I $3\overline{)29}$ T $9\overline{)87}$ A $5\overline{)45}$

R $8\overline{)63}$ E $2\overline{)20}$ B $3\overline{)72}$ F $4\overline{)76}$

___ ___ S S S S ___ ___ ___ ___
R1 R2   R6 R4 R7 R3

On another piece of paper, make up a code using remainders for your favorite subject in school.

Name _____

Wiggly Worms

Divide. Write each quotient in the puzzle.

Across

1. 5) 4,878

3. 2) 7,939

4. 8) 5,079

6. 7) 4,850

7. 6) 5,137

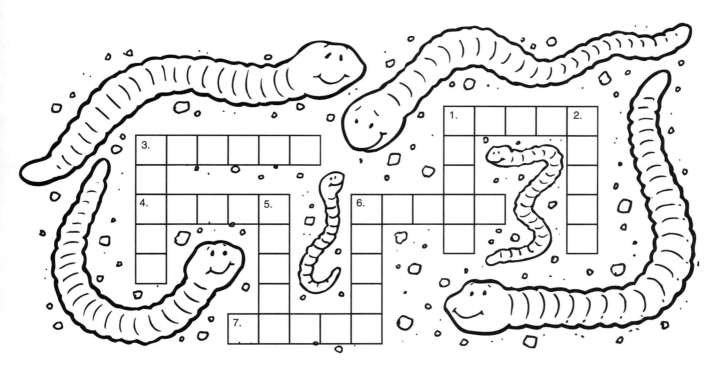

Down

1. 3) 2,968

2. 6) 1,909

3. 7) 2,708

5. 8) 6,077

6. 2) 1,359

There are 1,246 worms in the front yard. They are divided into 5 groups. How many worms are in each group? Are there any worms leftover?

Name _____

Spaceship Sweet Spaceship

Divide. Match each problem to its spaceship.

A.

$5 \overline{)2,568}$

B.

$9 \overline{)6,704}$

C.

$8 \overline{)7,546}$

D.

$3 \overline{)1,109}$

E.

$4 \overline{)3,543}$

F.

$6 \overline{)1,053}$

G.

$7 \overline{)5,027}$

H.

$9 \overline{)8,413}$

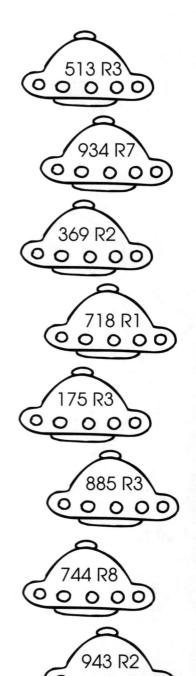

513 R3

934 R7

369 R2

718 R1

175 R3

885 R3

744 R8

943 R2

Write a division problem with your house or apartment number or zip code.

Name _____

Look Out from Below

Divide. Draw an **X** on each square with an odd-numbered remainder to stretch the periscope above the water.

A. 3) 206	B. 8) 6,356	C. 4) 31	D. 7) 334
E. 3) 29	F. 6) 5,072	G. 8) 68	H. 2) 1,713
I. 2) 197	J. 7) 6,690	K. 5) 4,476	L. 3) 3,502
M. 5) 48	N. 6) 400	O. 3) 4,049	P. 8) 4,316

On another piece of paper, write a division problem with an even-numbered remainder.

Name _____

Sweet Stuff

Remember to use a **decimal point** (.) and a **dollar sign** ($) or
a **cent sign** (¢) in the quotient when dividing with money.

Solve. Then, use the quotients to complete the price list.

A. Andrew Alien paid $6.51 for 7
   candy sticks. How much is a
   single candy stick?

B. Sam Space Creature paid $1.35
   for 5 gum balls. How much is one
   gum ball?

C. Alex Alien paid $7.84 for 8
   lollipops. How much is a single
   lollipop?

D. Sally Space Creature paid $8.64
   for 9 pieces of taffy. How much is
   one piece of taffy?

E. Molly Martian paid $2.37 for 3
   jawbreakers. How much is a
   single jawbreaker?

F. Mac Martian paid $5.78 for 2
   giant chocolate bars. How much
   is a single chocolate bar?

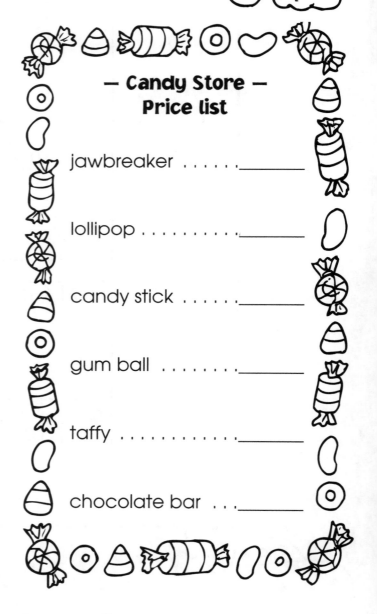

— Candy Store —
Price list

jawbreaker . . . . . . ._____

lollipop . . . . ._____

candy stick . . . . . ._____

gum ball . . . . ._____

taffy . . . . ._____

chocolate bar . . ._____

Pick your three favorite items on the list. Find the total amount.

Name _____

Riding the Wind

When dividing by two-digit divisors, begin by trying to divide into the first two digits of the dividend. If this number is not big enough, use the first three digits. Estimate how many times the divisor can go into that number. Then, multiply and subtract. Remember, if the difference is greater than the divisor, try a larger number in the quotient.

$$\begin{array}{r} 5 \\ 23\overline{)139} \\ -115 \\ \hline \textcircled{24} \end{array}$$

$$\begin{array}{r} 6\ R1 \\ 23\overline{)139} \\ -138 \\ \hline 1 \end{array}$$

$$\begin{array}{r} 6\ R1 \\ 23\overline{)139} \\ -138 \\ \hline 1 \end{array}$$

The difference is larger than the divisor. Try again.

Estimate which number on each kite would be the correct quotient. Divide.

A.
$$63\overline{)189}$$

B.
$$57\overline{)228}$$

C.
$$56\overline{)336}$$

D.
$$84\overline{)588}$$

E.
$$37\overline{)296}$$

F.
$$19\overline{)171}$$

G.
$$21\overline{)168}$$

H.
$$84\overline{)252}$$

Name _____

Heavy-Duty Division

Divide.

A.

$24\overline{)924}$ $17\overline{)235}$ $36\overline{)976}$ $18\overline{)371}$

B.

$22\overline{)463}$ $25\overline{)329}$ $19\overline{)366}$ $23\overline{)422}$

C.

$20\overline{)239}$ $33\overline{)678}$ $41\overline{)500}$ $54\overline{)407}$

D.

$20\overline{)704}$ $17\overline{)205}$ $19\overline{)223}$

Name _____

Digging Up Bones

Write **+**, **−**, **x**, or **÷** to complete each number sentence.

A. 4 ◯ 3 = 7   81 ◯ 9 = 9   6 ◯ 9 = 54

B. 8 ◯ 7 = 15   9 ◯ 3 = 6   7 ◯ 6 = 13

C. 7 ◯ 7 = 49   4 ◯ 2 = 8   3 ◯ 9 = 27

D. 21 ◯ 7 = 3   56 ◯ 8 = 7   10 ◯ 5 = 5

E. 8 ◯ 4 = 4   18 ◯ 12 = 6   12 ◯ 6 = 2

F. 36 ◯ 4 = 9   6 ◯ 6 = 36   11 ◯ 7 = 18

G. 6 ◯ 6 = 12   16 ◯ 4 = 12   7 ◯ 3 = 21

H. 48 ◯ 6 = 8   5 ◯ 5 = 25

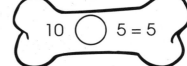

Word problems

Come to the Carnival

Circle the correct problem to solve each problem. Solve.

A.	There were 415 people who attended the school carnival. Of those, 316 rode the Ferris wheel. How many people did not ride the Ferris wheel?	$\begin{array}{r} 415 \\ + \ 316 \\ \hline \end{array}$ $\begin{array}{r} 415 \\ - \ 316 \\ \hline \end{array}$
B.	At the carnival, 236 people ate pink cotton candy, and 178 people ate blue cotton candy. How many people in all ate cotton candy?	$\begin{array}{r} 236 \\ + \ 178 \\ \hline \end{array}$ $\begin{array}{r} 236 \\ - \ 178 \\ \hline \end{array}$
C.	There were 23 rides at the carnival. If Whitney rode each ride 6 times, how many times did she ride in all?	$\begin{array}{r} 23 \\ + \ 6 \\ \hline \end{array}$ $\begin{array}{r} 23 \\ \times \ 6 \\ \hline \end{array}$
D.	There were 160 kids who played relay races at the carnival. The kids were divided into 8 teams. How many kids were on each team?	$\begin{array}{r} 160 \\ \times \ 8 \\ \hline \end{array}$ $8\overline{)160}$
E.	Carter sold 594 ride tickets in 1 hour at the carnival. How many tickets did he sell in 4 hours?	$\begin{array}{r} 594 \\ \times \ 4 \\ \hline \end{array}$ $4\overline{)594}$
F.	If 137 girls and 159 boys attended the carnival, how many more boys attended than girls?	$\begin{array}{r} 137 \\ + \ 159 \\ \hline \end{array}$ $\begin{array}{r} 159 \\ - \ 137 \\ \hline \end{array}$

Name _____

Fraction Fun

A **fraction** is a way to compare equal parts to a whole or a set.

> There are four parts to this whole or set.
> Two parts of the set are shaded.

The **denominator** is the bottom number of a fraction.
It tells the total number of equal parts in a whole or set.

The **numerator** is the top number of a fraction. It tells the number of equal parts being identified compared to the total number of equal parts in a whole or set.

The line separating the numerator and the denominator stands for "out of."

Write each fraction.

A.

____ out of ____ are cars $\dfrac{2}{9}$

____ out of ____ are trucks ____

____ out of ____ are motorcycles ____

B.

____ out of ____ are apples ____

____ out of ____ are bananas ____

____ out of ____ are pears ____

C.

____ out of ____ are baseballs ____

____ out of ____ are soccer balls ____

____ out of ____ are footballs ——

D.

____ out of ____ are triangles ____

____ out of ____ are circles ____

____ out of ____ are squares ——

Name _____

Which Is More?

Identify each fraction. Circle the greater fraction.

A.

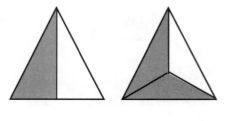

____ ____

B.

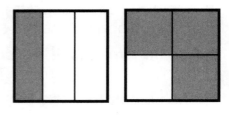

____ ____

C.

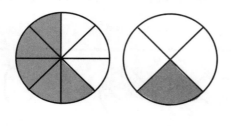

____ ____

D.

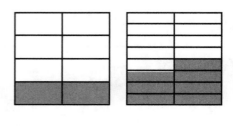

____ ____

E.

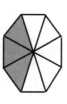

____ ____

F.

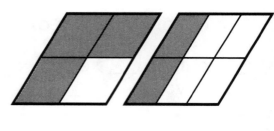

____ ____

G.

____ ____

H.

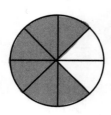

____ ____

Math Practice: Grades 3-4

Name _____

Measuring Cup Mix-Up

Use the fraction strips in the measuring cup to compare the fractions.

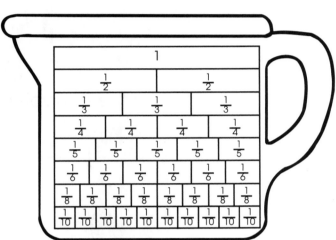

A. Circle the fraction that is less.

$\frac{1}{2}$	$\frac{2}{5}$
$\frac{2}{6}$	$\frac{2}{8}$
$\frac{4}{6}$	$\frac{3}{4}$
$\frac{4}{10}$	$\frac{1}{3}$

B. Circle the fraction that is greater.

$\frac{3}{6}$	$\frac{3}{5}$
$\frac{4}{8}$	$\frac{4}{5}$
$\frac{9}{10}$	$\frac{2}{3}$
$\frac{4}{10}$	$\frac{2}{6}$

Math Practice: Grades 3–4

Name _____

Just the Same

Equivalent fractions name the same amount of a set or whole.

 $\frac{1}{2}$ is equivalent to $\frac{3}{6}$.

A. Write each fraction. Draw a line to connect the equivalent fractions.

To find **equivalent fractions**, multiply the numerator and denominator by the same number.

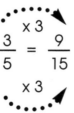
$$\frac{3}{5} = \frac{9}{15}$$

B. Multiply to find each equivalent fraction.

$$\frac{1}{2} = \frac{}{4} \qquad \frac{1}{3} = \frac{}{27} \qquad \frac{3}{4} = \frac{}{20} \qquad \frac{4}{6} = \frac{28}{} \qquad \frac{1}{7} = \frac{3}{}$$

Equivalent fractions can also be found by dividing the numerator and denominator by the same number.

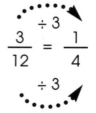
$$\frac{3}{12} = \frac{1}{4}$$

C. Divide to find each equivalent fraction.

$$\frac{4}{8} = \frac{}{4} \qquad \frac{15}{20} = \frac{3}{} \qquad \frac{4}{12} = \frac{2}{} \qquad \frac{14}{28} = \frac{2}{} \qquad \frac{18}{30} = \frac{}{5}$$

Math Practice: Grades 3–4

Name _____

Filling Up Bubbles

Each fish's bubbles are equivalent fractions. Fill in each missing fraction.

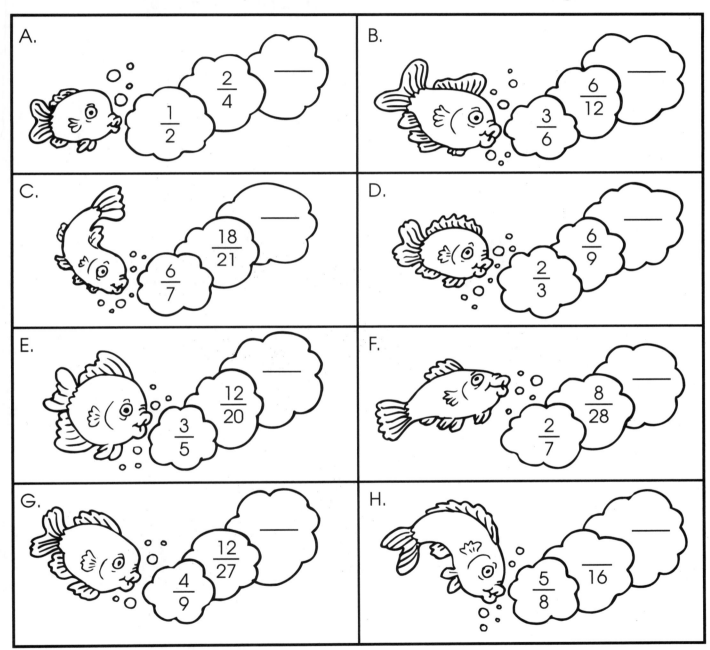

A. $\frac{1}{2}$ $\frac{2}{4}$ ____

B. $\frac{3}{6}$ $\frac{6}{12}$ ____

C. $\frac{6}{7}$ $\frac{18}{21}$ ____

D. $\frac{2}{3}$ $\frac{6}{9}$ ____

E. $\frac{3}{5}$ $\frac{12}{20}$ ____

F. $\frac{2}{7}$ $\frac{8}{28}$ ____

G. $\frac{4}{9}$ $\frac{12}{27}$ ____

H. $\frac{5}{8}$ $\frac{}{16}$ ____

Write 3 equivalent fractions for $\frac{2}{5}$. ____ , ____ , ____

Name _____

Keep It Simple

To put a fraction in **simplest form** means to rename or **reduce** the fraction without changing the amount.

Follow the steps to reduce a fraction.

$\frac{6}{9}$ 1. Find the largest number that can be divided into the numerator and denominator.

3   2. Both numbers can be divided by 3. $\frac{6}{9} \div \frac{3}{3} = \frac{2}{3}$

$\frac{2}{3}$ 3. The simplest form of $\frac{6}{9}$ is $\frac{2}{3}$.

 The two fractions still represent the same amount.

Reduce each fraction to simplest form.

A. $\frac{4}{10} \div = $ — $\frac{8}{32} \div = $ — $\frac{10}{12} \div = $ —

B. $\frac{18}{27} \div = $ — $\frac{5}{15} \div = $ — $\frac{4}{26} \div = $ —

C. $\frac{16}{56} \div = $ — $\frac{20}{45} \div = $ — $\frac{18}{40} \div = $ —

Name _____

Top Heavy

When the numerator is greater than or equal to the denominator, it is called an **improper fraction**.

$\dfrac{9}{4}$

When a whole number is with a fraction, it is called a **mixed number**.

$2\dfrac{1}{4}$

An improper fraction ($\dfrac{9}{4}$) can be changed to a mixed number.

Divide the numerator by the denominator.

$\dfrac{9}{4}$

$\begin{array}{r} 2\,R\,1 \\ 4\overline{)9} \\ -8 \\ \hline 1 \end{array}$

The quotient becomes the whole number. The remainder becomes a fraction. Use the denominator of the improper fraction.

$2\dfrac{1}{4}$

A mixed number ($2\dfrac{1}{4}$) can be changed to an improper fraction.

Multiply the whole number by the denominator.

$2\dfrac{1}{4}$ $2 \times 4 = 8$

Add the product to the numerator.

$8 + 1 = 9$

Write the sum over the original denominator.

$\dfrac{9}{4}$

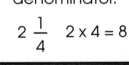

Change each improper fraction to a mixed number.

A. $\dfrac{14}{3} =$ $\dfrac{22}{7} =$ $\dfrac{44}{8} =$ $\dfrac{32}{5} =$

B. $\dfrac{13}{4} =$ $\dfrac{40}{6} =$ $\dfrac{18}{4} =$ $\dfrac{59}{9} =$

Change each mixed number to an improper fraction.

C. $1\dfrac{7}{8} =$ $2\dfrac{5}{9} =$ $4\dfrac{4}{7} =$ $7\dfrac{2}{6} =$

D. $2\dfrac{2}{5} =$ $2\dfrac{3}{5} =$ $6\dfrac{4}{9} =$ $3\dfrac{3}{4} =$

Math Practice: Grades 3–4

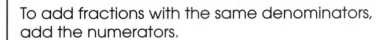
Nibble Away

To add fractions with the same denominators, add the numerators.

$$\frac{3}{10} + \frac{3}{10} = \frac{6}{10}$$

Reduce the answer to the simplest form.

$$\frac{6}{10} \div \frac{2}{2} = \frac{3}{5}$$

Add. Reduce to simplest form if needed. Circle the final answer.

A. $\frac{2}{18} + \frac{4}{18} =$ ___

B. $\frac{1}{5} + \frac{2}{5} =$ ___

C. $\frac{1}{8} + \frac{3}{8} =$ ___

D. $\frac{7}{32} + \frac{1}{32} =$ ___

E. $\frac{2}{7} + \frac{3}{7} =$ ___

F. $\frac{2}{10} + \frac{2}{10} =$ ___

G. $\frac{1}{4} + \frac{1}{4} =$ ___

H. $\frac{2}{6} + \frac{3}{6} =$ ___

I. $\frac{7}{11} + \frac{1}{11} =$ ___

J. $\frac{4}{15} + \frac{1}{15} =$ ___

K. $\frac{3}{25} + \frac{7}{25} =$ ___

L. $\frac{3}{12} + \frac{5}{12} =$ ___

M. $\frac{1}{3} + \frac{1}{3} =$ ___

N. $\frac{3}{9} + \frac{4}{9} =$ ___

Name _____

Pick a Peanut

To subtract fractions with the same denominators, subtract the numerators.

$$\frac{8}{10} - \frac{3}{10} = \frac{5}{10}$$

Reduce the answer to simplest form.

$$\frac{5}{10} \div \frac{5}{5} = \frac{1}{2}$$

Subtract. Reduce to simplest form if needed. Circle the final answer.

A.
$$\frac{4}{11} - \frac{2}{11} = \text{—}$$

B.
$$\frac{6}{9} - \frac{3}{9} = \text{—}$$

C.
$$\frac{4}{8} - \frac{1}{8} = \text{—}$$

D.
$$\frac{7}{10} - \frac{5}{10} = \text{—}$$

E.
$$\frac{6}{7} - \frac{3}{7} = \text{—}$$

F.
$$\frac{9}{12} - \frac{6}{12} = \text{—}$$

G.
$$\frac{4}{5} - \frac{2}{5} = \text{—}$$

H.
$$\frac{5}{6} - \frac{1}{6} = \text{—}$$

I.
$$\frac{3}{4} - \frac{1}{4} = \text{—}$$

J.
$$\frac{10}{12} - \frac{2}{12} = \text{—}$$

K.
$$\frac{11}{14} - \frac{4}{14} = \text{—}$$

L.
$$\frac{15}{25} - \frac{5}{25} = \text{—}$$

M.
$$\frac{8}{13} - \frac{6}{13} = \text{—}$$

N.
$$\frac{7}{15} - \frac{2}{15} = \text{—}$$

O.
$$\frac{5}{18} - \frac{1}{18} = \text{—}$$

Name _____

Something in Common

A **common denominator** is a multiple two denominators share.

A common denominator for $\frac{2}{5}$ and $\frac{4}{15}$ would be 15 because $5 \times 3 = 15$ and $15 \times 1 = 15$.

When adding fractions with different denominators, first find a common denominator. Then, change the fractions to equivalent fractions for adding.

Find a common denominator. Change to equivalent fractions.

Add.

Reduce to simplest form.

$$\frac{2}{5} \times \frac{3}{3} = \frac{6}{15}$$
$$+\frac{4}{15} \times \frac{1}{1} = \frac{4}{15}$$

$$\frac{6}{15} + \frac{4}{15} = \frac{10}{15}$$

$$\frac{10 \div 5}{15 \div 5} = \frac{2}{3}$$

Add. Reduce to simplest form.

A. $\frac{1}{2}$ $+\ \frac{3}{6}$	B. $\frac{2}{9}$ $+\ \frac{4}{36}$	C. $\frac{3}{7}$ $+\ \frac{2}{14}$
D. $\frac{4}{12}$ $+\ \frac{4}{36}$	E. $\frac{3}{9}$ $+\ \frac{1}{3}$	F. $\frac{1}{11}$ $+\ \frac{2}{22}$
G. $\frac{1}{3}$ $+\ \frac{5}{12}$	H. $\frac{3}{24}$ $+\ \frac{3}{6}$	I. $\frac{1}{20}$ $+\ \frac{4}{5}$

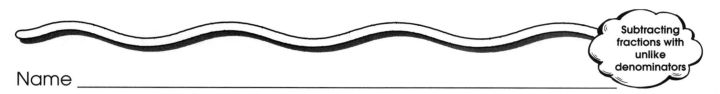

Name _____

Spaceship Satellite

When subtracting fractions with different denominators, first find a common denominator. Then, change the fractions to equivalent fractions for subtracting.

Find a common denominator. Subtract. Reduce to simplest form. Connect each satellite to the correct answer.

A. $\dfrac{1}{2} - \dfrac{3}{10} = $ ___

B. $\dfrac{2}{4} - \dfrac{10}{24} = $ ___

C. $\dfrac{6}{15} - \dfrac{1}{3} = $ ___

D. $\dfrac{13}{20} - \dfrac{3}{5} = $ ___

E. $\dfrac{6}{10} - \dfrac{2}{6} = $ ___

F. $\dfrac{5}{8} - \dfrac{7}{12} = $ ___

G. $\dfrac{7}{15} - \dfrac{7}{45} = $ ___

H. $\dfrac{5}{9} - \dfrac{10}{27} = $ ___

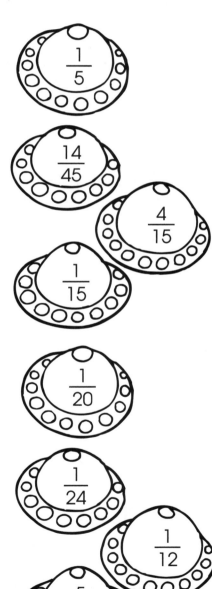

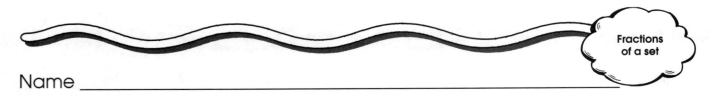

Name _____

Totally Bugged

Fractions can be used to identify part of a set.

There are 6 antennae. One-half ($\frac{1}{2}$) of the antennae is shaded. $\frac{1}{2}$ of 6 = 3

If you do not have a picture to find a fraction of a set, use division to help.

To find $\frac{1}{2}$ of 6, divide 6 by the denominator 2. Multiply 3 by the numerator 1.

$6 \div 2 = 3$ $3 \times 1 = 3$

One-half of six equals three.

To find $\frac{2}{3}$ of 24, divide 24 by the denominator 3. Multiply 8 by the numerator 2.

$24 \div 3 = 8$ $8 \times 2 = 16$

Two-thirds of twenty-four equals sixteen.

Solve each problem. Then, use the code to answer the riddle below.

T $\frac{2}{11}$ of 44 =

G $\frac{2}{7}$ of 49 =

A $\frac{2}{4}$ of 36 =

R $\frac{4}{6}$ of 48 =

S $\frac{3}{9}$ of 81 =

O $\frac{3}{12}$ of 24 =

n $\frac{2}{3}$ of 33 =

T $\frac{3}{4}$ of 20 =

A $\frac{1}{3}$ of 12 =

S $\frac{1}{2}$ of 18 =

What kind of bugs bother space creatures?

" $\overline{}$ $\overline{}$ $\overline{}$ $\overline{}$ $\overline{}$ $\overline{}$ $\overline{}$ $\overline{}$ $\overline{}$ $\overline{}$ "
  4   9   8   32   6   14   22   18   15   27

Name _____

What Is the Point?

A **decimal** is a number that uses a **decimal point** (.) to show tenths and hundredths instead of a fraction.

A **tenth** is one out of 10 equal parts of a whole.

A **hundredth** is one out of 100 equal parts of a whole.

  This picture can be written two ways.

1 $\frac{6}{10}$ (fraction)

1   $\frac{6}{10}$ 1.6   (decimal)

Write two ways to name each picture.

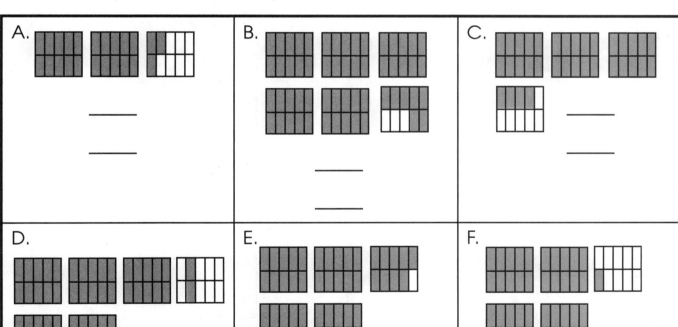

A. _____ _____

B. _____ _____

C. _____ _____

D. _____ _____

E. _____ _____

F. _____ _____

 Draw a picture to show 9.1.

Draw a picture to show 8 $\frac{6}{10}$.

95

Math Practice: Grades 3–4

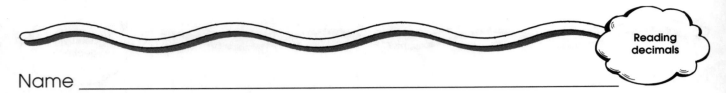

Name _____

Up, Up, and Away!

Decimals are read by looking at the place value.	whole number	and	tenths	hundredths
	4	.	6	8
	four and sixty-eight hundredths			

Read each decimal. Use numerals and decimal points to write it in the puzzle.

Across

1. four and eight tenths
3. two and six tenths
5. fourteen and twenty-three hundredths
6. one and twenty-two hundredths
7. seven and ninety-five hundredths
10. six and five tenths

Down

2. eight and six tenths
3. two and thirty-four hundredths
4. three and seventy-two hundredths
6. twelve and seven tenths
8. five and sixteen hundredths
9. nine and forty-five hundredths

Name _____

Astronomical Antennae

To compare decimals, first look at the whole numbers.

2.68 < 4.43   48.52 > 12.71

If the whole numbers are the same, compare the tenths.

7.83 > 7.38   80.74 > 80.07

If the whole number and the tenths are the same, compare the hundredths.

54.19 > 54.12   3.40 < 3.44

Use greater than > or less than < to compare each decimal. If the answer is greater than, shade the circle.

Write the decimals from least to greatest.

 _____, _____, _____, _____, _____, _____, _____, _____, _____,

_____, _____, _____, _____, _____, _____, _____, _____, _____

Name _____

Don't Forget Your Manners!

When adding or subtracting decimals, be sure to line up the decimal points. Remember to put the decimal point in the sum or difference.	$\begin{array}{r} 1 \\ 2.15 \\ +\ \ 4.68 \\ \hline 6.83 \end{array}$

Add or subtract. Then, use the code to answer the riddle below.

n	**R**	**W**	**T**	**B**	**F**	**E**
1.74 + 7.74	2.6 + 5.7	3.16 + 9.85	0.82 + 0.99	4.01 − 2.37	22.82 − 10.26	19.40 − 13.54

K	**S**	**H**	**y**	**O**	**A**	**C**
12.12 + 10.38	6.93 + 3.25	71.07 − 24.16	31.7 + 16.5	54.93 − 25.99	83.4 − 26.2	63.9 − 48.6

I	**L**
4.57 + 2.65	9.08 − 2.36

Why do octopuses have such a difficult time with table manners?

$\dfrac{}{1.81}$ $\dfrac{}{46.91}$ $\dfrac{}{5.86}$ $\dfrac{}{48.2}$ $\dfrac{}{15.3}$ $\dfrac{}{57.2}$ $\dfrac{}{9.48}$ $\dfrac{}{1.81}$, $\dfrac{}{22.50}$ $\dfrac{}{5.86}$ $\dfrac{}{5.86}$ $\overset{P}{\dfrac{}{}}$

$\dfrac{}{1.81}$ $\dfrac{}{46.91}$ $\dfrac{}{5.86}$ $\dfrac{}{7.22}$ $\dfrac{}{8.3}$ $\dfrac{}{5.86}$ $\dfrac{}{6.72}$ $\dfrac{}{1.64}$ $\dfrac{}{28.94}$ $\dfrac{}{13.01}$ $\dfrac{}{10.18}$ $\dfrac{}{28.94}$ $\dfrac{}{12.56}$ $\dfrac{}{12.56}$

$\dfrac{}{1.81}$ $\dfrac{}{46.91}$ $\dfrac{}{5.86}$ $\dfrac{}{1.81}$ $\dfrac{}{57.2}$ $\dfrac{}{1.64}$ $\dfrac{}{6.72}$ $\dfrac{}{5.86}$!

Graph It

> A **pictograph** uses symbols to show data.

Use the graphs to answer each question.

Mrs. Lopéz's class voted on favorite animals.

elephants	☺ ☺ ☺ ☺
sea lions	☺ ☺ ☺ ☺ ☺
birds	☺ ☺
snakes	☺ ☺ ☺ ☺ ☺ ☺

Each ☺ = 3 votes.

A. How many more students voted for sea lions than birds? _____

B. How many more students voted for snakes than elephants? _____

C. How many votes did elephants and birds receive altogether? _____

D. How many votes did sea lions and snakes receive altogether? _____

E. How many votes were recorded altogether? _____

> A **bar graph** uses bars to show data.

Concession Stand Sales

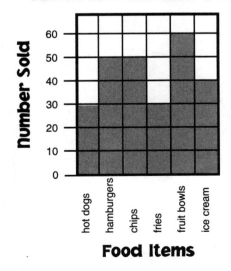

F. How many fruit bowls and ice-cream treats were sold altogether? _____

G. Which two items sold the least?

_____

H. Which item was sold the most?

_____

I. How many more hamburgers were sold than hot dogs? _____

J. How many more chips were sold than fries? _____

Name _____

Graph It Again

| A **line graph** connects points to show changes in data over time. |

Use the graphs to answer each question.

Caroline's Homework Time Chart

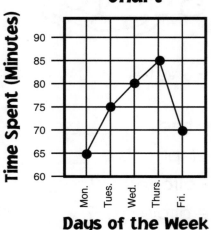

Time Spent (Minutes)

Days of the Week

A. Which day did Caroline spend the least amount of time on homework?

_____

B. Which day did Caroline spend the greatest amount of time on homework?

_____

C. How many more minutes did Caroline spend on homework on Wednesday than Friday?

_____

D. How many minutes did Caroline spend on homework for the week altogether?

_____

| A **circle graph** shows how the whole is broken into parts. |

E. Which activity was the most fun?

_____

F. Which activity was half as much fun as swimming? _____

G. Which activity was twice as much fun as movies?_____

H. Which two activities were the least fun?

_____

I. Which activity was as much fun as all the other activities combined? _____

Summer Fun

Name _____

Amazing Amusement Park

> A **grid** is a graph used to locate information. First, go to the letter. Then, go to the number.   **(A, 3)**

Write each item in the box using the given coordinates to make a map of the amusement park.

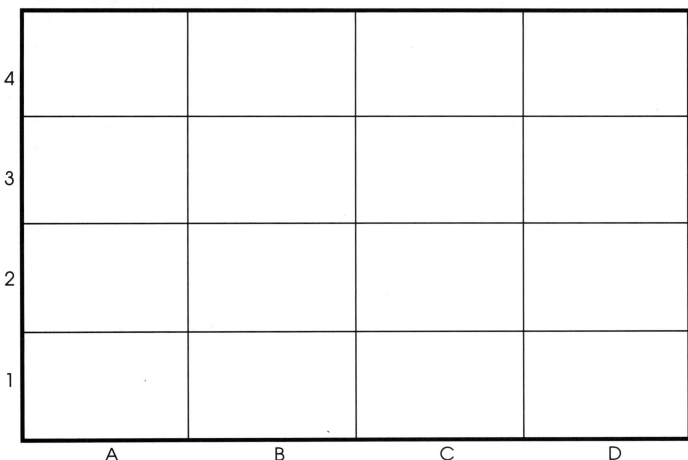

Park Entrance (A, 1)

Log Flume (D, 1) and (D, 2)

Ferris Wheel (B, 3)

Swings (C, 3)

Bumper Cars (A, 4)

Scrambler (D, 4)

Roller Coaster (B, 4) and (C, 4)

Merry-Go-Round (A, 3)

Snack Shop (D, 3)

Gift Shop (A, 2)

Train (B, 1), (B, 2), (C, 2), and (C, 1)

Name _____

Ride the Rides

Use the chart and table to answer each question.

Charts and tables are ways to organize data.

Wait Time

Ride	Minutes
roller coaster	15
log flume	22
scrambler	7
Ferris wheel	18
bumper cars	26

Number Times Ridden

	Clay	Trey	Joey	Tyler
log flume	18	15	20	14
roller coaster	24	18	11	31
scrambler	30	25	18	20
bumper cars	17	32	22	27
Ferris wheel	20	25	40	13

A. What ride has the shortest wait?
   _____

B. What ride has the longest wait?
   _____

C. How long is the wait for the roller coaster and Ferris wheel combined?_____

D. How much longer is the wait for the log flume than the scrambler?_____

E. How long is the wait to ride all rides?_____

F. If you only have 20 minutes, what rides can you choose from?

   _____

   _____

G. How many times did Clay ride the roller coaster and bumper cars combined? _____

H. How many more times did Trey ride the bumper cars than the log flume? _____

I. How many times did Joey and Tyler ride the scrambler altogether? _____

J. How many more times did Clay ride the roller coaster than Joey? _____

K. How many times did the boys ride the Ferris wheel altogether? _____

L. How many more times did the boys ride the Ferris wheel than the log flume? _____

Name _____

Time Flies

A. Write the time shown on each clock.

         (fourth clock)

____ : ____   ____ : ____   ____ : ____   ____ : ____

____ : ____   ____ : ____   ____ : ____   ____ : ____

B. Draw the hands on each clock for the time shown.

7:11   2:49   4:32   6:53

Draw the hands on each clock to show the start and end times. Write the elapsed time.

C.

The kids began making cupcakes at 9:30. At 11:45, all the cupcakes were ready to eat! How long did it take to prepare the cupcakes?

_____

D.

Lunch was served at 11:50. Everyone finished eating at 1:15. How long was the luncheon?

_____

Name _____

Day by Day

Time is measured by minutes, hours, days, weeks, months, and years. A **calendar** helps order the months of the year.

Answer each question using the February calendar.

A. How many Saturdays are there? _____

B. How many weeks are there? _____

C. How many days after the Spelling Bee is the math test? _____

D. What is the date one week after the report is due? _____

E. Draw an **X** on the third Monday.

February						
Sun.	Mon.	Tues.	Wed.	Thurs.	Fri.	Sat.
						1
2	3 Report Due	4	5	6	7	8 Carnival
9	10	11	12	13	♥ 14	15
16	17	Spelling 18 Bee	19	20	21	22
23	24	25	26	Math 27 Test	28	

F. Draw an **O** on the last Wednesday.

G. What is the date two weeks after the 6th? _____

H. What day of the week is the 20th? _____

How many months until your birthday? _____

What months have 30 days? _____

What months have 31 days? _____

What is the shortest month? _____

Name _____

Great Lengths

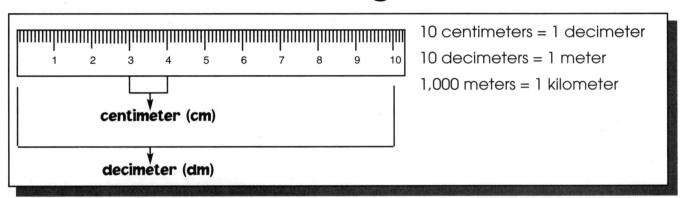

10 centimeters = 1 decimeter

10 decimeters = 1 meter

1,000 meters = 1 kilometer

A. Draw a line to connect the equal measurements.

4 km	40 cm
40 m	4 m
4 dm	4,000 m
400 cm	400 dm

B. Circle the best unit to measure the item in each picture.

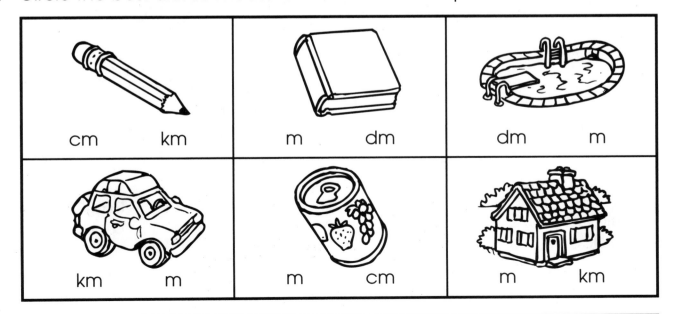

cm km	m dm
km m	m cm

dm   m
m   km

105

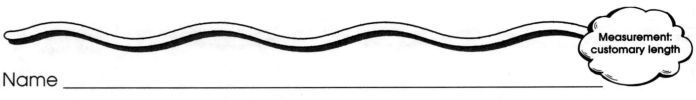

Name _____

Longing to Measure

12 inches	= 1 foot (ft.)
3 feet	= 1 yard (yd.)
5,280 feet	= 1 mile (mi.)
1,760 yards	= 1 mile (mi.)

Fill in the equal measurement for each.

A. 6 ft.   = _____ yd.

B. 48 in. = _____ ft.

C. 7 ft.   = _____ in.

D. 4 yd.   = _____ ft.

E. 36 in. = _____ yd.

Write the best unit to measure each item listed.

length of a driveway

_____

length of a camera

_____

height of a table

_____

height of a door

_____

length of a playground

_____

length of a swimming pool

_____

length of a book

_____

distance between two cities

_____

height of a person

_____

Name _____

Light as a Feather

Mass is the amount of matter something contains.

1 gram (g)	1 kilogram (kg)

1,000 grams = 1 kilogram

Use the items circled to complete the puzzle.

Across		**Down**	
Circle each item which would be measured in kilograms.		Circle each item with the least mass.	
2. flowerpot	sock	1. marble	chair
4. television	comb	2. flower	scooter
5. pencil	desk	3. towel	case of soda
6. cracker	bike	6. bed	banana

Name _____

Heavy as a Rock

16 ounces (oz.) = 1 pound (lb.)	2,000 pounds (lb.) = 1 ton (T.)

A. Draw a line to the best unit of measure.

ounce

pound

ton

B. Use **>**, **<**, or **=** to compare the measurements.

16 oz. ◯ 2 lb.   3 T. ◯ 5,000 lb.   2 lb. ◯ 35 oz.

1 T. ◯ 1,000 lb.   70 oz. ◯ 4 lb.   18 oz. ◯ 1 lb.

C. Circle each item measured in pounds.
Find the remaining words backward in
the puzzle.

person   watermelon   bike

house   tractor   table

cherries   truck   boat

computer

a	q	v	k	r	e
f	d	t	a	o	b
j	r	g	z	t	c
h	b	f	u	c	i
p	m	e	l	a	t
w	e	s	x	r	o
k	c	u	r	t	d
i	s	o	h	y	n
c	m	h	b	g	a

Name _____

Cook's Questions

 = 1 cup (c.)

= 1 pint (pt.)

= 1 quart (qt.)

= 1 gallon (gal.)

Circle the two measurements in each row that are the same.

A.

B.    3 cups   1 quart

C.   1 gallon   3 quarts   8 pints

D.   6 pints   1 gallon   4 quarts

Do you have enough? Circle **yes** or **no**.

	You have	You need	Enough	
E.	3 c.	1 pt.	YES	NO
F.	4 pt.	1 qt.	YES	NO
G.	8 pt.	1 gal.	YES	NO
H.	1 qt.	3 pt.	YES	NO
I.	6 c.	2 qt.	YES	NO
J.	1/2 gal.	3 pt.	YES	NO

Name _____

Moving Mercury

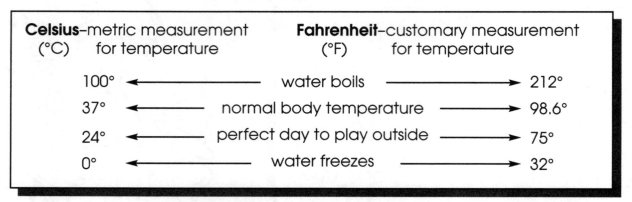

Celsius–metric measurement		**Fahrenheit**–customary measurement	
(°C) for temperature		(°F) for temperature	
100° ⟵	water boils	⟶	212°
37° ⟵	normal body temperature	⟶	98.6°
24° ⟵	perfect day to play outside	⟶	75°
0° ⟵	water freezes	⟶	32°

Write each temperature.

A. 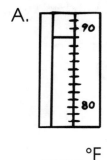   B. 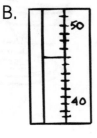   C. 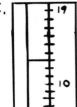   D. 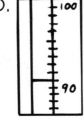   E.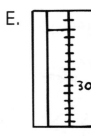

____ °F   ____ °C   ____ °C   ____ °F   ____ °F

Write the temperature for each picture.

F.

____ °C ____ °F

G.

____ °C ____ °F

H.

____ °C ____ °F

I.

____ °C ____ °F

Math Practice: Grades 3–4

Name _____

In Great Shape

A **spatial figure** has length, width, height, and volume.

The **face** is the flat side of a spatial figure.

Connect each figure with its name. Then, connect each name with the number of faces it has.

Figure	**Name**	**Number of Faces**
A.	pyramid	1
B.	cube	6
C.	cylinder	5
D.	cone	0
E.	sphere	2
F.	rectangular prism	6

Classify each item by its shape. Complete the chart to classify each item.

marble

party hat

cereal box

globe

straw

block

die   candle

pyramid

soccer cone

cube	rectangular prism
pyramid	cone
cylinder	sphere

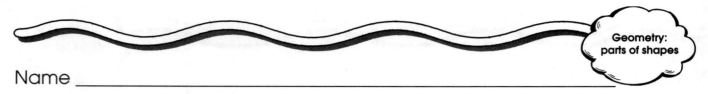

Name _____

That's a Great Line

A **line segment** is part of a line that has two end points.

Endpoints are at either end of a line segment or at the start of a ray.

An **angle** consists of two line segments with a common endpoint.

Parallel lines are lines that do not intersect.

Closed curves are lines that connect with no endpoint.

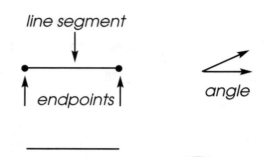

line segment

endpoints

angle

parallel lines

closed curve

Write the number of parts in each shape.

A. ____ line segments

____ endpoints

____ angles

parallel lines?   Y   N

closed curves?   Y   N

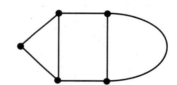

B. ____ line segments

____ endpoints

____ angles

parallel lines?   Y   N

closed curves?   Y   N

 On another piece of paper, draw a shape with a closed curve and three angles.

C. ____ line segments

____ endpoints

____ angles

parallel lines?   Y   N

closed curves?   Y   N

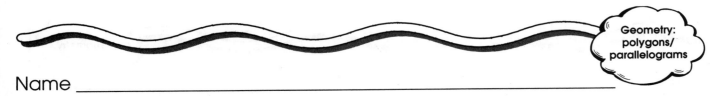

Name _____

Everything Is Closed

A **polygon** is a closed plane figure made of line segments.

A polygon with three sides is a **triangle**.

A polygon with four sides is a **quadrilateral**.

A polygon with five sides is a **pentagon**.

Use the code to color each shape.

Color Code

triangles: red

quadrilaterals: white

pentagons: blue

A.

B.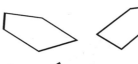

C.

A **parallelogram** is a quadrilateral with two pairs of opposite parallel sides.

Finish the parallelogram patterns.

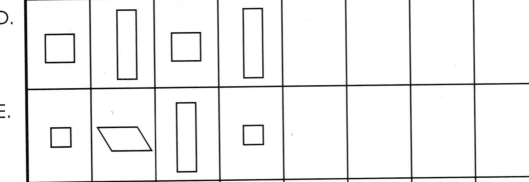

Name _____

Alien Angled Antennae

A **right angle** is an angle that forms a square corner.

An **acute angle** is an angle that is less than a right angle.

An **obtuse angle** is an angle that is greater than a right angle.

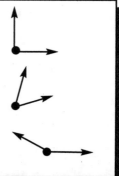

Write the name for each alien's antennae angle.

A.

_____ _____ _____ _____

B.

_____ _____ _____ _____

C.

_____ _____ _____ _____

 On another piece of paper, draw an alien with two sets of acute angle antennae.

114 Math Practice: Grades 3–4

Name _____

Twin Figures

Congruent figures are those that are the same size and shape, regardless of the shape's direction. The change in direction is called movement, and there are three types.

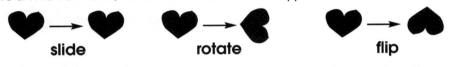

slide   rotate   flip

Circle the congruent shapes in each row.

A.

B.

C.

D.

 Draw a set of congruent shapes.

Name _____

Side by Side

Symmetrical figures are those that have two sides that match exactly when split in half.

A line of **symmetry** is a line that divides a figure into two identical parts.

Some figures have one line of symmetry. Some figures have two lines of symmetry.

Draw one line of symmetry on each figure. Draw an **X** on each figure without symmetry.

A. 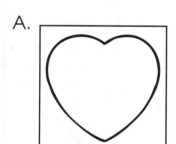 B. 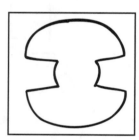 C.  D.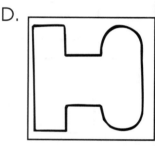

E.  F.  G. 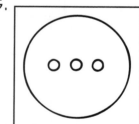 H.

I.  J. 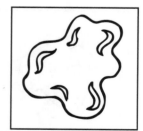 K.  L.

 There are two figures with two lines of symmetry. Circle these figures and draw the second line of symmetry.

Name _____

Perimeter Pathway

The **perimeter** is the distance around a closed figure. To find the perimeter, measure each side of the figure and add all the sides together.

Add to find the perimeter of each figure.

A. 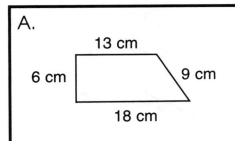 perimeter = ____ cm	B. 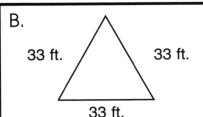 perimeter = ____ ft.	C. 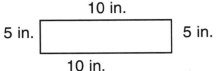 perimeter = ____ in.
D. 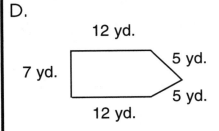 perimeter = ____ yd.	E. 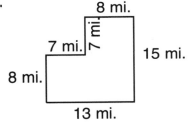 perimeter = ____ mi.	F. 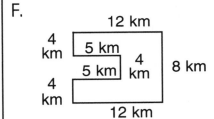 perimeter = ____ km

G.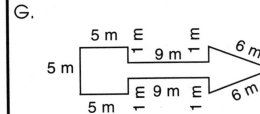

perimeter = ____ m

H.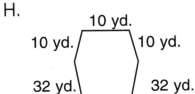

perimeter = ____ yd.

 Find the perimeter of your room in feet. Find the perimeter of your favorite book in centimeters.

Name _____

Under Cover

Area is the number of square units needed to cover the surface of a closed figure.

To find the area of a figure, multiply the two sides of that figure.

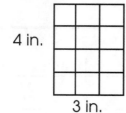

4 in.

3 in.

4 in. x 3 in. = 12 square inches

area = 12 square inches

Find the area of each room in the house.

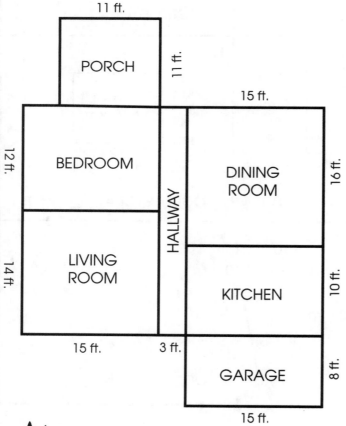

11 ft.

PORCH

11 ft.

15 ft.

12 ft.

BEDROOM

14 ft.

LIVING ROOM

HALLWAY

DINING ROOM

16 ft.

KITCHEN

10 ft.

15 ft.   3 ft.

GARAGE

8 ft.

15 ft.

A. garage   A = _____ sq. ft.

B. kitchen   A = _____ sq. ft.

C. dining room A = _____ sq. ft.

D. hallway   A = _____ sq. ft.

E. living room A = _____ sq. ft.

F. bedroom   A = _____ sq. ft.

G. porch   A = _____ sq. ft.

Find the area of your bedroom in square feet.

Name _____

Party Packages

Volume is the number of cubic units needed to fill a solid figure.

To find the volume of a figure, multiply the length by the width by the height.

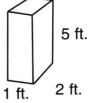

5 ft.

1 ft.   2 ft.

2 ft. x 1 ft. x 5 ft. = 10 cubic ft.

volume = 10 cubic feet

Find the volume of each present.

A. 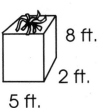 8 ft. 2 ft. 5 ft. volume = _____ cu. ft.	B. 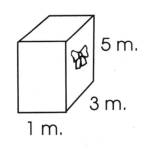 5 m. 3 m. 1 m. volume = _____ cu. m	C. 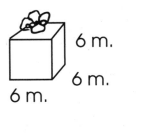 6 m. 6 m. 6 m. volume = _____ cu. m.

D. Find the volume of each part of the cake. Then, find the total volume.

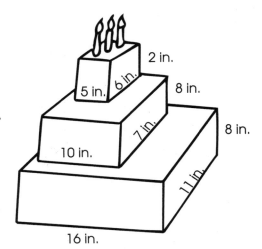

bottom layer   = _____ cu. in.

middle layer   = _____ cu. in.

+   top layer   = _____ cu. in.

total volume = _____ cu. in.

2 in.

5 in. 6 in. 8 in.

10 in. 7 in. 8 in.

16 in. 11 in.

Name _____

A Pocket Full of Change

When counting money, always begin with the coin with the greatest value.

Math Practice: Grades 3-4

Name _____

Thank You, Come Again!

List the money needed using the least amount of dollars and coins.

Amount Needed	$1	25¢	10¢	5¢	1¢
A. $4.97					
B. $.53					
C. $1.66					
D. $.84					
E. $.28					
F. $2.89					
G. $3.17					
H. $2.70					
I. $6.47					

Name _____

Time to Review

Fill in the circle that completes the fact family.

1. $6 \times 3 = 18$
    $3 \times 6 = 18$ (A) $18 \div 9 = 2$ (B) $6 + 3 = 9$ (C) $18 \div 3 = 6$ (D) $18 - 6 = 12$
    $18 \div 6 = 3$

2. Divide.

    A. $4\,\overline{)\,68}$ $5\,\overline{)\,295}$ $4\,\overline{)\,59}$ $6\,\overline{)\,971}$

    B. $8\,\overline{)\,5{,}963}$ $2\,\overline{)\,7{,}599}$ $7\,\overline{)\,4{,}368}$ $63\,\overline{)\,260}$

3. A family of five bought sodas for each person. They paid $12.75. How much did each soda cost?

4. Write the correct symbol to complete each number sentence.

    A. $72 \bigcirc 9 = 8$ B. $7 \bigcirc 7 = 14$

    C. $12 \bigcirc 2 = 10$ D. $6 \bigcirc 7 = 42$

5. Reduce to simplest form.

    A. $\dfrac{8}{36} = $ _____   B. $\dfrac{3}{21} = $ _____

Name _____

6. Change each improper fraction to a mixed number.

   A. $\dfrac{13}{2}$ =   B. $\dfrac{23}{5}$ =   C. $\dfrac{37}{6}$ =

7. Change each mixed number to an improper fraction.

   A. $5\dfrac{2}{7}$ =   B. $3\dfrac{1}{8}$ =   C. $7\dfrac{1}{10}$ =

8. Add. Reduce to simplest form.

   A. $\dfrac{3}{6} + \dfrac{4}{10}$ B. $\dfrac{5}{7} + \dfrac{3}{14}$

9. Subtract. Reduce to simplest form.

   A. $\dfrac{13}{45} - \dfrac{2}{9}$ B. $\dfrac{7}{8} - \dfrac{5}{8}$

10. Solve.

   A. $\dfrac{2}{7}$ of 35   B. $\dfrac{2}{3}$ of 66

11. Write the decimal.

    _____

12. Write the time.

  _____

13. Write 2 hours and 15 minutes later.

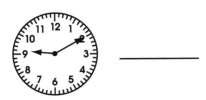

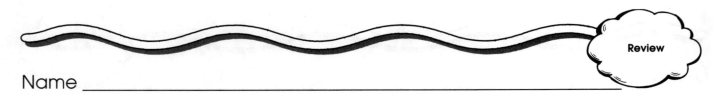
14. Select the best unit of measure.

A.   Ⓐ mi.   Ⓑ ft.   Ⓒ in.

B.   Ⓐ m   Ⓑ km   Ⓒ cm

15.

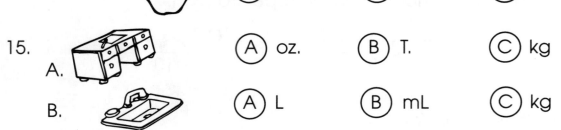

A.   Ⓐ oz.   Ⓑ T.   Ⓒ kg

B.   Ⓐ L   Ⓑ mL   Ⓒ kg

16. Choose the shape that is not congruent.

Ⓐ   Ⓑ   Ⓒ   Ⓓ

17. Which shape does not have a line of symmetry?

Ⓐ   Ⓑ   Ⓒ   Ⓓ

18. Find the perimeter.

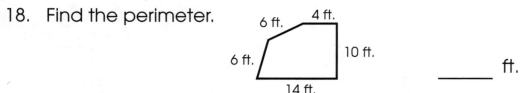

6 ft.   4 ft.

6 ft.   10 ft.

14 ft.

_____ ft.

19. Which figure has the greatest area?

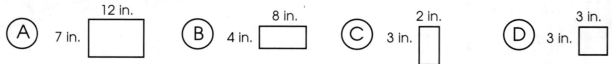

12 in.
Ⓐ 7 in. ▭

8 in.
Ⓑ 4 in. ▭

2 in.
Ⓒ 3 in. ▯

3 in.
Ⓓ 3 in. ▯

20. Which figure has a volume of 288 cubic yards?

Ⓐ 4 yd. 4 yd. 4 yd.   Ⓑ 3 yd. 4 yd. 12 yd.   Ⓒ 12 yd. 8 yd. 3 yd.   Ⓓ 3 yd. 3 yd. 3 yd.

21. Count the coins.

_____

Page 4
A. 4th, 5th, 6th, 7th; B. 15th, 16th, 17th, 18th; C.49th, 50th, 51st, 52nd, 53rd; D. 95th, 93rd, 92nd, 90th, 89th; E. 79th; 78th, 76th, 75th, 74th; 9; 16

Page 5
Check students' drawings.; 3

Page 6
A. 22; B. 94; C. 70; D. 51; E. 86; F. 33; G. 8; H. 44; 8 tens 3 ones

Page 7
A. 245; B. 503; C. 162; D. 338; E. 294; F. 376

Page 8
A. 4,130; B. 1,448; C. 3,513; D. 5,095

Page 9
A. 2,000 + 500 + 80 + 7 = 2,587; B. 4,000 + 200 + 50 + 1 = 4,251; C. 1,000 + 300 + 40 + 4 = 1,344; D. 6,000 + 100 + 0 + 3 = 6,103; E. 5,000 + 700 + 60 + 2 = 5,762; F. 3,000 + 500 + 10 + 0 = 3,510; G. 9,000 + 400 + 70 + 5 = 9,475; H. 7,000 + 0 + 30 + 6 = 7,036; I. 8,000 + 600 + 50 + 0 = 8,650; 9,475; 7,036; 6,103

Page 10

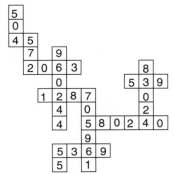

Page 11
A. 22, 23, 25, 26, 27; B. 311, 310, 308, 307, 305; C. 653, 651, 650, 649, 648; D. 1,868; 1,870; 1,871; 1,873; E. 49,429; 49,430; 49,433; 49,434; 49,435; F. 531, 530, 528, 527; G. 246; 383; 5,307; 89,264; H. 80,689; 5,150; 4,297; 4,178

Page 12
even: 52; 6,314; 59,870; 148; 42,936; 75,244; odd: 71,343; 8,685; 97; 359; 569,271; 845; even, even, odd

Page 13
A. 20; 570; 7,080; B. 26,500; 800; 4,100; C. 874,000; 56,000; 2,000; D. 900,000; 70,000; 40,000; E. 700,000; 500,000; 700,000

Page 14

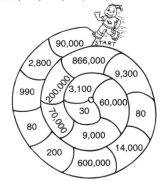

Page 15
A. >, =, >; B. >, <, >; C. >, <, >; D. >, >, >; E. <, =, >; F. <, <, >; 4

Page 16

536	519	180	242	376
291	100	587	912	511
307	352	475	145	237
486	732	609	946	468
147	86	813	100	299

532	498	477	561	590
512	732	313	234	694
575	486	493	504	483
176	853	467	946	559
515	509	525	577	493

48,566	63,103	46,053	53,197	68,310
75,234	42,035	86,000	80,273	74,299
50,246	66,041	53,076	42,100	76,000
43,707	42,026	41,283	56,248	79,245
76,122	76,135	79,201	41,999	76,129

8,907	11,251	10,762	9,341	10,566
11,175	8,901	8,254	11,287	8,943
10,244	11,276	8,903	8,873	9,762
8,914	11,627	11,342	11,269	9,425
9,240	10,560	11,250	10,015	10,617

ASTROKNOTS

Page 17

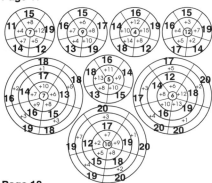

Page 18
8 = c; 10 = h; 6 = p; 17 = t; 12 = n; 3 = s; 15 = e; 5 = y; 14 = k; 19 = f; 9 = b; 11 = m; 20 = a; 13 = q; 18 = g; 2 = i; 4 = r; 7 = d; 16 = o; 19 = l; THEY NEEDED A GOOD BATTER!

Page 19
R. 59; I. 74; C. 99; P. 64; E. 99; A. 79; T. 97; A. 95; P. 89; G. 85; P. 89; T. 67; C. 77; G. 96; R. 88; T. 85; C. 99; R. 78; PRICE TAG

Page 20
A. 94, 91, 104, 90, 66, 90, 64; B. 90, 91, 104, 84, 104, 63, 101; C. 91, 100, 81, 85, 81, 95, 74

Page 21
A. 791, 570, 671, 962, 891, 890; B. 1,091, 986, 983, 792, 856, 882; C. 772, 672, 833, 984, 950, 890

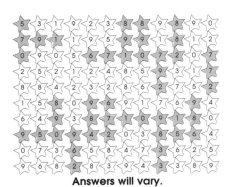

Answers will vary.

Page 22

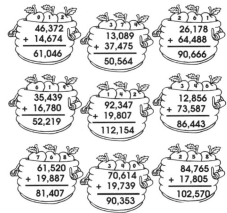

	435	814	601	660
723	623	900	901	1,010	602
356	823	461	504	844	935
910	923	753	1,402	1,701	1,122
830	640	913	1,025	872	1,241
1,282	1,070	1,613	1,223	723	953

Page 23
T. 5,969; H. 6,099; A. 5,605 C. 6,992; K. 8,650; F. 9,484; D. 9,793; N. 10,680; 7,465; O. 7,865; A. 9,889; O. 9,195; T. 5,993; E. 6,427; A. 8,582; W. 10,444; AT THE CROAK OF DAWN!

Page 24
A. 5,810; 8,630; 7,920; 5,773; 6,940; B. 2,803; 4,801; 9,801; 8,801; 7,801; C. 9,902; 9,843; 9,860; 9,932; 7,487; D. 5,248; 8,517; 7,519; 9,519; 8,518

Page 25
A. 10,200; C. 8,305; S. 4,425; E. 6,033; R. 11,320; T. 9,400; I. 8,101; M. 8,214; K. 5,024; H. 6,004; ARITHMETRICKS

Page 26
J. 73,615; R. 93,916; M. 97,192; Y. 52,445; S. 65,980; T. 102,856; P. 52,846; O. 91,581; I. 52,467; H. 91,869; U. 81,935; ! 85,198; YOU SHIP IT!

Page 27

46,372 + 14,674 = 61,046	13,089 + 37,475 = 50,564	26,178 + 64,488 = 90,666
35,439 + 16,780 = 52,219	92,347 + 19,807 = 112,154	12,856 + 73,587 = 86,443
61,520 + 19,887 = 81,407	70,614 + 19,739 = 90,353	84,765 + 17,805 = 102,570

Page 28
Across: 1. 86,143; 4. 94,406; 6. 44,003; 7. 32,073; 9. 57,130; 10. 42,000; Down: 1. 81,445; 2. 35,014; 3. 82,303; 5. 63,043; 8. 70,520

Page 29
A. 5,743; R. 4,386; U. 9,318; C. 2,681; E. 6,800; A. 5,977; S. 3,928; R. 6,975; P. 10,715; M. 6,908; X. 8,280; O. 7,195; O. 4,297; L. 3,235; D. 5,062; F. 3,176; A CAR POOL

Page 30
A. 25, 32, 21, 22; B. 70, 33, 31, 21; C. 13, 22, 35, 2; D. 43, 20, 23, 10

Page 31
G. 59; S. 36; D. 38; A. 64; M. 29; C. 28; L. 19; J. 68; W. 45; B. 29; N. 17; O. 18; R. 27; H. 29; D. 27; E. 14; SWORDFISH

Page 32
A. 149, 292, 183, 473, 474, 483; B. 661, 188, 229, 315, 226, 580; C. 242, 294; D. 271, 361; E. 705, 184; F. 362, 393

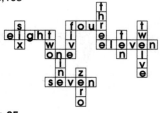

Page 33
K. $1.88; Y. $1.77; E. $1.89; B. $3.84; I. $3.79; R. $2.65; C. $4.39; O. $1.79; S. $4.59; U. $2.88; T. $3.77; H. $3.89; YOU STRIKE IT RICH!

Page 34
Across: 3. 2,424; 5. 2,835; 8. 2,117; 9. 1,089; 12. 2,077; Down: 1. 2,183; 2. 6,523; 3. 5,132; 4. 1,712; 6. 6,291; 7. 2,810; 10. 5,976; 11. 3,105

Page 35
A. 3,196; 3,407; 3,978; ones increase by 1; B. 3,253; 2,385; 2,907; odd numbers; C. 2,364; 2,774; 2,089; tens increase by 1; D. 1,989; 2,929; 3,219; thousands increase by 1

Page 36
C. 2,889; M. 3,588; E. 1,886; T. 5,829; U. 6,747; S. 5,867; A. 4,089; P. 1,596; D. 2,976; H. 2,865; B. 5,589; K. 1,889; I. 5,788; G. 5,868; N. 3,799; O. 4,777; THE HOOPING COUGH

Page 37

31,909 yellow	43,249 red	32,919 red	13,719 yellow
41,728 blue	23,189 yellow	12,387 yellow	43,728 green
15,828 blue	43,915 yellow	43,188 yellow	57,168 green
38,209 yellow	35,633 orange	27,626 orange	18,610 yellow

Page 38
A. 53,069; B. 37; C. 22,420; D. 13,218; E. 16,789; F. 42,529; G. 22,457; H. 23,458; 396,844

Page 39
A. 27,869; 58,785; B. 7,879; 27,888; C 28,782 18,789; 57,839; 38,883; D. 3,588; 15,879; 17,882; 28,382

Page 40
S. 275; A. 479; R. 392; N. 278; B. 2,283; O. 369; I. 28,130; U. 18,109; C. 9,759; T. 227; SUB-TRACTION

Page 41
A. 227; 494; B. 658; 2,467; C. 3,525; 3,645; D. 34,838; 25,785; E. 3,532; 4,423; F. 24,567; 10,784

Page 42
A. $12.38; B. $1.63; C. 58¢; D. $5.12; E. yes; F. $5.25; 4

Page 43
A. 8,10,12,16,18, 20, 22; B.15, 25, 30, 40, 45, 50; C. 12, 16, 24, 28, 36; D. 12, 15, 18, 21, 27, 30; E. 24, 30, 42, 48, 60; F. 27, 36, 45, 63, 81, 90; G. 32, 40, 48, 64, 72; H. 21, 28, 35, 56, 63, 70

Page 44
A. 2 + 2 + 2 + 2 = 8, 4 sets of 2 equals 8, 4 x 2 = 8; B. 4 + 4 + 4 = 12, 3 sets of 4 equals 12, 3 x 4 = 12; C. 5 + 5 + 5 + 5 + 5 = 25, 5 sets of 5 equals 25, 5 x 5 = 25; D. 3 + 3 + 3 + 3 + 3 + 3 = 18, 6 sets of 3 equals 18, 6 x 3 = 18

Page 45
A. 6, 3,18, 6 x 3 = 18; B. 2, 4, 8, 2 x 4 = 8; C. 5, 7, 35, 5 x 7 = 35; D. 3, 8, 24, 3 x 8 = 24; E. 4, 11, 44, 4 x 11 = 44; F. 4, 12, 48, 4 x 12 = 48

Page 46

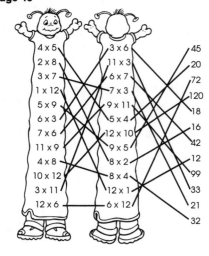

Page 47
A. 14, 24, 8, 16, 10, sum = 72, green; B. 10, 25, 40, 15, 45, sum = 135; C. 40, 90, 100, 30, 50, sum = 310, yellow; D. 64 ,56, 88, 24, 40, sum = 272; E. 16, 36, 48, 20, 12, sum = 132; F. 72, 24, 66, 48, 42, sum = 252; G. 27, 108, 72, 54, 18, sum = 279; H. 36, 21, 33, 18, 27, sum = 135; I. 56, 84, 49, 42, 63, sum = 294; J. 36, 84, 72, 60, 48, sum = 300; K. 99, 44, 22, 77, 66, sum = 308

Page 48

10	40	0	120	54	21
24	11	25	20	56	81
36	9	84	0	16	16
66	24	24	30	80	48
63	6	88	49	20	3
15	16	36	48	0	60

Page 49

X	0	1	2	3	4	5	6	7	8	9	10	11	12
0	0	0	0	0	0	0	0	0	0	0	0	0	0
1	0	1	2	3	4	5	6	7	8	9	10	11	12
2	0	2	4	6	8	10	12	14	16	18	20	22	24
3	0	3	6	9	12	15	18	21	24	27	30	33	36
4	0	4	8	12	16	20	24	28	32	36	40	44	48
5	0	5	10	15	20	25	30	35	40	45	50	55	60
6	0	6	12	18	24	30	36	42	48	54	60	66	72
7	0	7	14	21	28	35	42	49	56	63	70	77	84
8	0	8	16	24	32	40	48	56	63	72	80	88	96
9	0	9	18	27	36	45	54	63	72	81	80	99	108
10	0	10	20	30	40	50	60	70	80	90	100	120	120
11	0	11	22	33	44	55	66	77	88	99	110	121	132
12	0	12	24	36	48	60	72	84	96	108	120	132	144

B. 0, 0, 5, 0; C. even, odd, even

Page 50
A. 7; M. 4; T. 2; E. 8; Q. 6; S. 1; U. 0; I. 9; R. 3; TIMES SQUARE

Page 51
A. 36, 531; B. 644, 423; C. 332, 81; D. 32, 416; E. 465, 152; F. 553, 72; G. 332, 465; H. 432, 384; I. 528, 390; 24, 60, 96, 48, 84

Page 52

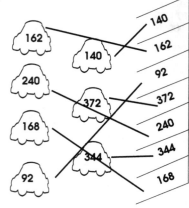

 is the top decorative border.

Page 53
A. 384; 1,641; 870; 648; 1,540; B. 1,108; 2,976; 5,216; 2,592; 940; C. 3,772; 2,388; D. 1,714; 1,491; E. 2,180; 4,344; F. 7,624; 5,523; G. 7,758; 2,895

Page 54
A. $3.51; B. $8.56; C. $4.70; D. $18.65; E. $13.84; F. $25.34; G. $23.31; H. $38.82

Page 55
Across: 1. 54,252; 3. 47,115; 4. 22,188; 6. 39,775; 8. 20,880; 9. 28,536; Down: 2. 24,612; 4. 25,388; 5. 8,388; 7. 46,188; 8. 22,432

Page 56
A. 42 x 21 = 882; 33 x 32 = 1,056; 15 x 11 = 165; 44 x 22 = 968; B. 24 x 21 = 504; 31 x 23 = 713; 12 x 23 = 276; 23 x 13 = 299; C. 33 x 22 = 726, 20 x 10 = 200, 30 x 13 = 390, 41 x 22 = 902

Page 57
E. 3,256; K. 2,660; J. 2,134; A. 6,396; W. 3,588; R. 4,732; S. 1,081; B. 8,366; E. 2,688; A. 5,025; JAWBREAKERS

Page 58
A. 432; F. 3,034; S. 2,925; Y. 2,400; G. 1,292; L. 3,480; C. 2,772; E. 2,910; I. 3,724; U. 3,588; N. 1,645; R. 2,970; A FLYING SAUCER

Page 59
A. 11,537; 48,316; 20,097; B. 79,016; 11,675; 4,764; C. 56,000; 17,100; 38,064; D. 36,498; 31,535; 39,788; E. 9,867; 24,732; 27,938

Page 60
P. 26,348; U. 44,096; B. 62,522; O. 25,678; E. 26,100; R. 30,784; N. 21,560; L. 6,164; I. 19,768; W. 25,862; S. 43,197; A. 36,271; IN A "SUPER" BOWL

Page 61
1. C; 2. B; 3. 2,380; 4. 65,500; 5. 258,000; 6. A; 7. B; 8. 9; 9. 7; 10. 13; 11. 20

Page 62
12. 452; 13. 6,406; 14. 76,041; 15. 37,761; 16. 59; 17. 385; 18. 2,765; 19. 443

Page 63
20. 663; 21. 6,466; 22. 148; 23. 684; 24. 4,656; 25. 57,663; 26. 3,230; 27. 26,095; 28. 13,344; 29. 35,993

Page 64
A. 16, 4, 4, 16 ÷ 4 = 4; B. 12, 4, 3, 12 ÷ 4 = 3; C. 70, 7, 10, 70 ÷ 7 = 10; D. 15, 3, 5, 15 ÷ 3 = 5

Page 65
A. 2; B. 3; C. 10; D. 2; E. 1; F. 4; G. 3, 6; H. 6, 24

Page 66
A. 7 x 3 = 21; 3 x 7 = 21; 21 ÷ 3 = 7; 21 ÷ 7 = 3; B. 6 x 8 = 48, 8 x 6 = 48, 48 ÷ 6 = 8, 48 ÷ 8 = 6; C. 8 x 7 = 56; 7 x 8 = 56; 56 ÷ 8 = 7; 56 ÷ 7 = 8; D. 9 x 4 = 36; 4 x 9 = 36; 36 ÷ 9 = 4; 36 ÷ 4 = 9; E. 4 x 5 = 20; 5 x 4 = 20; 20 ÷ 5 = 4; 20 ÷ 4 = 5; F. 9 x 2 = 18; 2 x 9 = 18; 18 ÷ 9 = 2; 18 ÷ 2 = 9; G. 8 x 3 = 24; 3 x 8 = 24; 24 ÷ 8 = 3; 24 ÷ 3 = 8; H. 7 x 5 = 35; 5 x 7 = 35; 35 ÷ 5 = 7; 35 ÷ 7 = 5

Page 67
A. 8; B. 6; C. 8; D. 7; E. 8; F. 3; G. 8; H. 9; 1. 5; J. 7; K. 4; L. 5; M. 5; N. 9; O. 7; P. 8; Q. 2; R. 7; S. 7

Page 68
A. 4, 7, 9, 9, 7; B. 11, 6, 6, 2, 9; C. 7, 9, 10, 5, 4; D. 1, 4, 12, 7, 3; 24 ÷ 4 = 6 cookies

Page 69

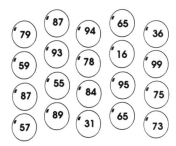

Page 70
E. 163; R. 134; L. 197; B. 139; E. 169; H. 178; U. 176; A. 459; W. 297; B. 264; L. 238; B. 269; WHALE BLUBBER

Page 71
A. 3,978; B. 1,479; C. 2,645; D. 1,274; E. 1,869; F. 1,244; G. 2,839; H. 1,947; I. 1,423

Page 72

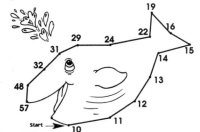

Page 73
A. 72, 136, 175, 225; B. 101, 115, 60, 181; C. 34, 96, 95, 236; D. 89, 43, 34, 74

Page 74
H. 9 R1; K. 5 R5; O. 9 R4; Y. 7 R3; L. 6; I. 9 R2; T. 9 R6; A. 9; R. 7 R7; E. 10; B. 24; F. 19; HISTORY

Page 75
Across: 1. 975 R3; 3. 3,969 R1; 4. 634 R7; 6. 692 R6; 7. 856 R1; Down: 1. 989 R1; 2. 318 R1; 3. 386 R6; 5. 759 R5; 6. 679 R1; 249 worms, 1 worm left over

Page 76
A. 513 R3; B. 744 R8; C. 943 R2; D. 369 R2; E. 885 R3; F. 175 R3; G. 718 R1; H. 934 R7

Page 77

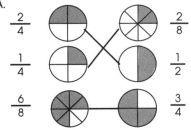

68 R 2	794 R4	7 R4	47 R5
9 R2	845 R2	8 R4	856 R1
98 R1	955 R5	895 R1	1,167 R1
9 R3	66 R4	1,349 R2	539 R4

Page 78
A. 93¢; B. 27¢; C. 98¢; D. 96¢; E. 79¢; F. $2.89

Page 79
A. 3; B. 4; C. 6; D. 7; E. 8; F. 9; G. 8; H. 3

Page 80
A. 38 R12, 13 R14, 27 R4, 20 R11; B. 21 R1, 13 R4, 19 R5, 18 R8; C. 11 R19, 20 R18, 12 R8, 7 R29; D. 35 R4, 12 R1, 11 R14

Page 81
A. +, ÷, x; B. +, –, +; C. x, x, x; D. ÷, ÷, –; E. –, –, ÷; F. ÷, x, +; G. +, –, x; H. ÷, x

Page 82
A. 99; B. 414; C. 138; D. 20; E. 2,376; F. 22

Page 83
A. 2, 9, 3, 9, 3/9, 4, 9, 4/9; B. 3, 12, 3/12, 5, 12, 5/12, 4, 12, 4/12; C. 2, 15, 2/15, 6, 15, 6/15, 7, 15, 7/15; D. 8, 18, 8/18, 4, 18, 4/18, 6, 18, 6/18

Page 84
Bolded fractions should be circled. A. 1/2, **2/3**; B. 1/3, **3/4**; C. **5/8**, 1/4; D. 2/8, **7/16**; E. **3/8**, 1/4; F. **3/4**, 2/6; G. **1/2**, 1/4; H. 1/3, **6/8**

Page 85
A. 2/5, 2/8, 4/6, 1/3; B. 3/5, 4/5, 9/10, 4/10

Page 86
A.

2/4 · · 2/8

1/4 · · 1/2

6/8 · · 3/4

B. 2, 9, 15, 42, 21; C. 2, 4, 6, 4, 3

Page 87
Answers will vary. Possible answers include: A. 4/8; B. 12/24; C. 54/63; D. 18/27; E. 48/80; F. 32/112; G. 36/81; . 20/32; 4/10, 6/15, 8/20

Page 88
A. 2, 2/5, 8, 1/4, 2, 5/6; B. 9, 2/3, 5, 1/3, 2, 2/13; C. 8, 2/7, 5, 4/9, 2, 9/20

Page 89
A. 4 2/3, 3 1/7, 5 4/8, 6 2/5; B. 3 1/4, 6 4/6, 4 2/4, 6 5/9; C. 15/8, 23/9, 32/7, 44/6; D. 12/5, 13/5, 58/9, 15/4

Page 90
A. 6/18 = 1/3; B. 3/5; C. 4/8 = 1/2; D. 8/32 = 1/4; E. 5/7; F. 4/10 = 2/5; G. 2/4 = 1/2; H. 5/6; I. 8/11; J. 5/15 = 1/3; K. 10/25 = 2/5; L. 8/12 = 2/3; M. 2/3; N. 7/9

Page 91
A. 2/11; B. 3/9 = 1/3; C. 3/8; D. 2/10 = 1/5, E. 3/7; F. 3/12 = 1/4; G. 2/5; H. 4/6 = 2/3; I. 2/4 = 1/2; J. 8/12 = 2/3; K. 7/14 = 1/2; L. 10/25 = 2/5; M. 2/13; N. 5/15 = 1/3; O. 4/18 = 2/9

Page 92
A. 6/6 = 1; B. 12/36 = 1/3; C. 8/14 = 4/7; D. 16/36 = 4/9; E. 6/9 = 2/3; F. 4/22 = 2/11; G. 9/12 = 3/4; H. 15/24 = 5/8; I. 17/20

Page 93
A. 2/10 = 1/5; B. 2/24 = 1/12; C. 1/15; D. 1/20; E. 8/30 = 4/15; F. 1/24; G. 4/45; H. 5/27

Page 94
T. 8; G. 14; A. 18; R. 32; S. 27; O. 6; N. 22; T. 15; A. 4; S. 9; ASTROGNATS

Page 95
A. 2 3/10, 2.3; B. 5 7/10, 5.7; C. 3 4/10, 3.4; D. 7 2/10, 7.2; E. 6 9/10, 6.9; F. 4 1/10, 4.1

Page 96
Across: 1. 4.8; 3. 2.6; 5. 14.23; 6. 1.22; 7. 7.95; 10. 6.5; Down: 2. 8.6; 3. 2.34; 4. 3.72; 6. 12.7; 8. 5.16; 9. 9.45

Page 97

Page 98
N. 9.48; R. 8.3; W. 13.01; T. 1.81; B. 1.64; F. 12.56; E. 5.86; K. 22.50; S. 10.18; H. 46.91; Y. 48.2; O. 28.94; A. 57.2; C. 15.3; I. 7.22; L. 6.72; THEY CAN'T KEEP THEIR ELBOWS OFF THE TABLE!

Page 99
A. 9; B. 6; C. 18; D. 33; E. 51; F. 100; G. hot dogs and fries; H. fruit bowls; I. 20; J. 20

Page 100
A. Monday; B. Thursday; C. 10; D. 375; E. swimming; F. sleeping late; G. reading; H. trips and movies; I. swimming

Page 101

4	Bumper Cars	Roller Coaster		Scrambler
3	Merry-Go-Round	Ferris Wheel	Swings	Snack Shop
2	Gift Shop	Train		Log Flume
1	Park Entrance			
	A	B	C	D

Page 102
A. scrambler; B. bumper cars; C. 33 minutes; D. 15 minutes; E. 88 minutes; F. roller coaster, scrambler, Ferris wheel; G. 41; H. 17; I. 38; J. 13; K. 98; L. 31

Page 103
A. 1:27, 11:13, 8:38, 3:46; 5:07, 9:12, 1:51, 12:39; B. Check students' clocks.; C. 2 hr. 15 min.; E. 1 hr. 25 min.

Page 104
A. 4; B. 4; C. 9; D. Feb. 10; E. Feb. 17; F. Feb. 26; G. Feb. 20; H. Thursday

Page 105
A. 4 km = 4,000 m, 40 m = 400 dm, 4 dm = 40 cm, 400 cm = 4 m; B. cm, dm, m, m, cm, m

Page 106
A. 2 yd.; B. 4 ft.; C. 84 in.; D. 12 ft.; E. 1 yd.; Answers will vary.

Page 107

Page 108
A. ounce = popcorn, pound = apples, ton = car; B. <, >, <, >, >, >; C. person, watermelon, bike, table, cherries, computer

Page 109
A. 2 cups, 1 pint; B. 2 pints, 1 quart; C. 1 gallon, 8 pints; D. 1 gallon, 4 quarts; E. yes; F. yes; G. yes; H. no; I. no; J. yes

Page 110
A. 89°F; B. 46°C; C. 13°C; D. 91°F; E. 37°F; F. 100°C, 212°F; G. 24°C, 75°F; H. 0°C, 32°F; I. 37°C, 98.6°F

Page 111
A. cube, 6; B. cone, 1; C. rectangular prism, 6; D. cylinder, 2; E. sphere, 0; F. pyramid, 5; cube: die, block; rectangular prism: cereal box; pyramid: pyramid; cone: party hat, soccer cone; cylinder: straw, candle; sphere: marble, globe

Page 112
A. 3, 4, 2, no, yes; B. 6, 5, 7, yes, yes; C. 4, 4, 4, yes, yes

Page 113
A. red, red, white, blue; B. blue, red, blue, white; C. red, white, blue, white;

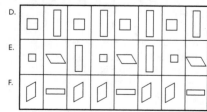

Page 114
A. obtuse, acute, right, right; B. acute, right, acute, acute; C. right, obtuse, acute, obtuse

Page 115
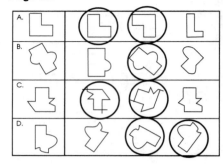

Page 116
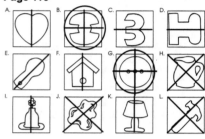

Page 117
A. 46; B. 99; C. 30; D. 41; E. 56; F. 50; G. 49; H. 102

Page 118
A. 120; B. 150; C. 240; D. 78; E. 210; F. 180; G. 121

Page 119
A. 80; B. 15; C. 216; D. 1408, 560, 60, total volume = 2028

Page 120
A. 25¢; B. 76¢; C. 42¢; D. 71¢; E. 43¢; F. 51¢; G. 75¢; H. 57¢; I. 29¢

Page 121

	Change needed	$1	25¢	10¢	5¢	1¢
A.	$4.97	4	3	2		2
B.	$.53		2			3
C.	$1.66	1	2	1	1	1
D.	$.84		3		1	4
E.	$.28		1			3
F.	$2.89	2	3	1		4
G.	$3.17	3		1	1	2
H.	$2.70	2	2	2		
I.	$6.47	6	1	2		2

Page 122
1. C; 2. A. 17, 59, 14 R3, 161 R5; B. 745 R3, 3,799 R1, 624, 4 R8; 3. $2.55; 4. A. ÷, B. +, C. −, D. x; 5. A. 2/9, B. 1/7

Page 123
6. A. 6 1/2, B. 4 3/5, C. 6 1/6; 7. A. 37/7, B. 25/8, C. 71/10; 8. A. 9/10, B. 13/14; 9. A. 1/15, B. 1/4; 10. A. 10, B. 44; 11. 2.3; 12. 11:38; 13. 11:25

Page 124
14. A. ft.; B. cm; 15. A. kg; B. kg; 16. B; 17. A; 18. 40 ft.; 19. A; 20. C; 21. 86¢